EXCELLER SELECT

TOP PICKS

CHASING HORIZONS

AF516557

CHASING HORIZONS

Memoirs of an Air Force Brat

Gautam Chakraborty

EXCELLER BOOKS®
A GLOBAL PRESS

Chasing Horizons
Memoirs of an Air Force Brat

Copyright © Gautam Chakraborty, India, 2025

Cover by Exceller Books

All rights reserved. No portion of the book may or should be reproduced, stored in any retrieval system (including but not limited to computers, disks, external drives, electronic or digital devices, e-readers, websites), or transmitted in any form or by any means (mechanical, recording, electronic, digital version, photocopying, or otherwise) without the prior, written permission of the publisher, nor be otherwise circulated in any form of binding or cover other than that in which it is published and without a similar condition being imposed on the Subsequent purchaser.

The book has been published with all reasonable efforts taken to make the material error-free after the consent of the author. The views and opinions expressed in this book are the author's own and the facts are as reported by him. Neither the publisher nor editor endorse or approve the content of this book or guaranty the reliability, accuracy or completeness of the content published herein and do not make and representations of warranties of any kind, express or implied, including but not limited to the implied warranties of merchantability, fitness for a particular purpose. The publisher or editor shall not be liable whatsoever for any errors, omissions, whether such errors or omissions result from negligence, accident or any other cause or claims for loss or damage of any kind, including without limitation damage arising out of use, or about reliability, accuracy, sufficiency of the information contained in this book.

ISBN: 978-93-47397-72-1

Published in India in 2025 by Exceller Books,
An imprint of GE Group,
G1, Dream Apartment, Degree College Road, Belgharia,
Kolkata, 700056, India
www.excellerbooks.com

EXCELLER BOOKS®
A GLOBAL PRESS

Dedicated to

(Late) Warrant Officer Dilip Kumar Chakraborty (IAF)

My father, guide and spiritual guru, who keeps holding my hands and helping me with life's choices, in his lifetime and after—physically and spiritually!

Prologue

The deafening roar of a fighter jet still makes me look up instinctively, even decades later. It's funny how some things become hardwired into your system when you grow up on Air Force bases. That sound—part mechanical scream, part thunderclap—was the soundtrack of my childhood, as usual to me as birdsong is to others.

Welcome to my world—or rather, my worlds, plural. I've lived so many lives in one lifetime that sometimes I wonder if I'm actually several people masquerading as a single human. Air Force brat, reluctant student, accidental revolutionary, desert wanderer, and eventually, a man trying to make sense of it all. This memoir is my attempt to stitch these fragments into something resembling a coherent story.

I should warn you upfront: I'm about to share some deeply embarrassing moments alongside the profound ones. There's the time I nearly drowned trying to fish a cockroach out of floodwater with a broom (age five, not my finest strategic thinking). Or when my friend and I became campus legends at college by claiming a tiny "island" in the middle of a flooded field, complete with an umbrella and a stool, while professors and students gathered at windows to watch the spectacle. Dignity was clearly not my strong suit.

My earliest memories are framed by the barbed-wire link fences of Air Force stations across India—Delhi's bustling Palam, coastal Jamnagar, conflict-torn Amritsar, strategic Adampur, historic Ambala, and the scorching deserts of Bikaner. Our family bounced between military quarters that reflected my father's modest rank as an aircraft maintenance technician. These homes were temporary by design, but the constant relocations taught me that home isn't a geographical location but a portable feeling you carry within.

Those tiny quarters, often surrounded by tall grass where neighbourhood dogs would chase unsuspecting children (namely me), became theatres for my earliest adventures. I once fled in terror from a dog, running faster than my small legs had ever carried me before, inevitably tripping and falling. As I rolled in panic, expecting teeth and pain, I instead got curious sniffing from a dog that was more interested than aggressive. First life lesson: fear and reality often exist in entirely different dimensions—something that would serve me well throughout life, where perceived dangers and actual risks rarely aligned.

Military bases exist as curious microcosms—neither entirely military nor completely civilian, governed by regulations yet teeming with humanity's full spectrum. I witnessed security guards who dined squatting on mess floors, only using tables during inspections. I marvelled at wild Holi celebrations where usually disciplined personnel transformed into unrecognisable, jubilant revellers. These festivals offered glimpses of the humans behind uniforms, revealing personalities usually concealed beneath khaki and insignia.

Nothing compared to the thrill of watching fighter jets roar overhead while we waved frantically at pilots from our school playground. Sometimes, helicopter pilots would wave back, creating electric connections between earth and sky that made us feel chosen. We'd debate afterwards whether the wave had been directed at one specific student or intended as a general greeting, each of us claiming personal connection to these aviators who represented the pinnacle of military prestige.

Picture this: a six-year-old boy falling head over heels for his classmate, showing off swimming prowess at the Air Force pool just to catch her eye. This wasn't just any childhood crush—this was serious business involving strategic planning worthy of a military operation. At the tender age of seven, I mustered all my courage to dive from the deep end—a feat few peers attempted—secretly hoping she was watching. That same romantic would spend the next decade secretly hoping to run into her again during our nomadic military postings across India, but alas...I never did find her again. Isn't that how the best childhood crushes remain perfect—preserved in memory precisely because they never evolved into complicated reality?

As I grew older, my sheltered Air Force childhood began to intersect with broader national tensions. In Amritsar, I witnessed Operation Bluestar from our windows, watching soldiers crawl across melting asphalt while bullets and rockets whizzed overhead. At Adampur, our annual school function abruptly ended when the principal announced Prime Minister Indira Gandhi's assassination. Later that evening, as Rajiv Gandhi lit his mother's funeral pyre on our small black-and-white television, an inexplicable scent of sandalwood wafted through our living room—as though national grief had transcended physical boundaries to reach us.

My teenage years at Ambala brought new dimensions to this military-civilian hybrid identity. Joining the Air Wing of the National Cadet Corps provided structure and purpose that resonated with my upbringing. The pinnacle came when I attended a ten-day Annual Training Camp at Sainik School, Kunjpura—being among the select few conferred special privileges, including parade boots with horseshoes clipped to the heels—a distinction that left me with painful corns that persist to this day, a physical reminder of my connection to that proud teenage cadet.

Despite demonstrating aptitude in Mathematics and Science, my true intellectual passion emerged in History and Literature. I became fascinated by ancient civilisations of Africa and America, feeling moral outrage at how Western approaches had systematically erased these cultural achievements. The history of the Russian Revolution captured my imagination, and I began collecting Soviet books, dreaming with like-minded friends about creating a more just society in India.

Then came the seismic shifts of 1989-90, when my romantic revolutionary ideals collided with historical reality as communist regimes collapsed across Eastern Europe. This intellectual crisis coincided with my academic stumble at the end of school, when I failed Chemistry and barely passed with 50% overall. What initially felt like a catastrophe turned out to be serendipity, freeing me to pursue Economics and English Literature in college.

College represented my first genuine immersion in civilian space—a world where military hierarchy held no sway. I discovered the exhilarating disorientation of freedom: bunking classes to watch "Aashiqui" with classmates (only to discover our entire class had the same idea); claiming that ridiculous island in the flooded college grounds; participating in anti-Mandal Commission protests that revealed both the power and moral complexity of collective action.

The most profound influence on my worldview during this period came from Richard Bach's "Jonathan Livingston Seagull"—initially appealing for its aviation themes but ultimately meaningful for its exploration of spiritual dimensions and the quest for perfection. The college library became my sanctuary—a place where ideas could be explored without the immediate practical applications demanded by Air Force life.

After just one year of college, my father received transfer orders to Bikaner. Before departing, my college friend and I embarked on a final adventure—a trip to Shimla, my first experience visiting mountainous terrain. Standing on a wooden balcony, watching the sunset paint distant peaks with what my fourth-standard Hindi textbook had called "molten gold," I couldn't have imagined the stark contrast awaiting me in Bikaner's blazing desert, where temperatures inside tanks at Mahajan reportedly reached 67°C (152.6°F).

The desert presented its own lessons in extremes—scorching days followed by surprisingly cool nights, the rigid social hierarchies of Rajasthani society contrasting with the fluid rank-based structure of military life. I found myself at a crossroads between military service and management education, ultimately choosing the latter path despite the persistent pull of the uniform that had defined my childhood identity.

This memoir traces not just geographical movements but internal transformations—how a child raised under fighter wings developed a worldview balancing structure with spontaneity, respect for hierarchy with healthy scepticism toward authority. You'll witness how military life shaped not just external circumstances but my inner landscape, creating someone who felt simultaneously part of an elite community and perpetually an outsider in civilian contexts.

Negotiating the twists and turns of my growing-up years, I always felt a nagging pull of conscience, trying to hold me down to the elusive roots I was always chasing, living through the duality of romance and reality. In one moment of poetic inspiration and still a novice in the world of poetry, I penned my feelings thus:

Romance-Reality-Mirage

A sweet little boy
Opened his eyes
And saw the world.
It was beautiful!
He saw the bright moon
Shining over the beautiful valley, and
The fairies beckon him
From behind the clouds
Floating lazily above.
Then he turned around and
Saw another boy
With dirty, dark skin and rickety legs
Clinging to the hanging breasts
Of a walking corpse. His mother.
The boy stepped into his youth
And looked around,
He saw himself

With his sweetheart in his arms
Gazing dreamily into the waterfall
Besides the mountains;
He kissed the forehead of his beloved
Under the glowing moon
And felt the silky hairs
Billowing in the breeze.
Suddenly, he turned around
And saw a tycoon
Seated in his Mercedes
Toss a coin
To the rickety boy and his mother
Then drive past them
Splashing the boy and his mother
With the roadside filth.
The boy became a young man
And found himself among a distinguished crowd
Receiving a prestigious award
For the prize-winning photograph
Of the rickety boy and his mother.
He heard himself talking
Of existentialism and
Upliftment of the proletariat.
Lazily, he peeked out of the window
And saw the rickety boy sobbing
Besides the corpse,
His mother!

I invite you into a world where national events and personal milestones collide, where a military brat transforms through corporate rate-race and development finance, from scorching deserts to misty mountains—this is the story of finding your centre when everything shifts, and discovering that life's most beautiful trajectories emerge when your flight path gets gloriously disrupted.

So, fasten your seatbelts! There might be some turbulence ahead, but I promise the view will be worth it. After all, the best stories, like the best flights, aren't always the smoothest, but they take you to places you'll never forget.

Contents

Chapter 1

Chasing Horizons: Early Years in the Shadow of Wings

The Rhythm of Change

My earliest memories date back to the mid and late 1970s, a time when India was undergoing rapid transformation. The Emergency had just ended, colour television was still a luxury few could afford, and Ambassador cars dominated our roads. Yet within the high-security fences of Air Force stations, life maintained its own distinct rhythm and traditions, insulated mainly from civilian upheavals.

Growing up as an Air Force kid during this period meant embracing one constant: change. From Delhi's Air Force station Palam with its bustling activity and proximity to the capital's pulse, to the coastal airbase at Jamnagar in Gujarat, where fighter jets created daily soundtracks to our lives, our family bounced between military quarters and modest civil accommodations that reflected my father's humble paycheck as an aircraft maintenance technician.

Our homes changed frequently—sometimes annually—but the backdrop of roaring fighters and military life remained, creating a strange paradox of instability and consistency that military children everywhere might recognise. We lived in a world where packing up an entire household became routine, where friendships were formed with the understanding that they might be temporary, and where the sight of moving trucks triggered not distress but excitement about new adventures ahead.

Those tiny quarters, often surrounded by tall grass where neighbourhood dogs would chase an unsuspecting child (namely me), became the stage for my earliest adventures and misadventures alike. The standard-issue military housing wasn't exactly spacious—typically a single bedroom for a family of four. But what these quarters lacked in luxury, they made up for in community. Neighbours weren't just people who lived next door; they were extended family who watched your children, shared meals during festivals, and understood the unique challenges of service life without explanation.

I vividly recall one heart-pounding incident when, while playing amidst the tall grass surrounding our quarters at Palam, a dog began chasing me. Not just any dog, mind you, but what my terrified seven-year-old mind registered as a massive, snarling beast (though in retrospect, it was probably a medium-sized mutt). Terror propelled my small legs faster than they'd ever moved before, my lungs burning as I sprinted toward home. But inevitably, I tripped and fell, tumbling dramatically into the grass like a shot-down aircraft.

As I began rolling in panic, expecting teeth and pain at any moment, I instead experienced the curious sniffing of a dog that was perhaps more interested than aggressive. The fearsome predator of my imagination turned out to be a relatively friendly stray, more puzzled by my theatrical panic than intent on making me its dinner. This moment, like many others, taught me that fear and reality often exist in different dimensions—a lesson that would serve me well throughout life in military environments where perceived dangers and actual risks weren't always aligned.

My father would later use this incident as a teaching moment, explaining that many threats in life appear more dangerous from a distance than they actually are when confronted directly—a philosophy that helped me navigate everything from school bullies to later professional challenges. It was one of many impromptu life lessons delivered between aircraft maintenance shifts, often while he polished his uniform buttons or pressed his clothes for the next day's duty.

First Love and Lasting Impressions

Picture this: a six-year-old boy falling head over heels for his classmate, showing off his swimming prowess at the Air Force pool just to catch her eye. This wasn't just any childhood crush—this was serious business that involved strategic planning and performance worthy of a military operation. To my young eyes, she embodied perfection—short "Sadhna-cut" hair adorned with ribbons that matched her school uniform, and a smile that transformed ordinary school days into occasions of significance.

I can't remember when exactly I first noticed her—perhaps during morning assembly at Kendriya Vidyalaya, Jamnagar, or maybe during one of the countless cultural functions where she performed *Rabindra Nritya* (dances on Rabindranath Tagore's songs, mixing Bengali folk and Manipuri classical dance styles) with a grace that seemed supernatural to my besotted heart. What I do remember is the immediate and overwhelming conviction that she was the most important person in my small universe, a feeling that persisted with embarrassing intensity throughout my primary school years.

The Kendriya Vidyalaya (Central School) at Air Force Station, Jamnagar, like most schools in military environments, emphasised both academic achievement and physical activities. During cultural programs and annual functions, students performed dances, recited poetry, and participated in dramatic productions. I would eagerly cheer her during school dance performances, positioning myself so she might notice my enthusiastic support, and applauding with excessive vigour when she completed her choreographed movements. These cultural events became highlights of my school year, not for their intrinsic entertainment value but for the opportunities they provided to observe my lady love in settings beyond the classroom.

I recited poetry with extra enthusiasm during competitions, hoping she'd be impressed by my oratorical skills and confidence on stage. When I won first place in an inter-class recitation contest with a theatrical rendition of "Where the Mind is Without Fear" by Rabindranath Tagore, I scanned the audience immediately for her reaction, valuing her approving nod more than the certificate presented by the principal. The fact that she probably had no idea I was performing specifically for her did nothing to diminish my romantic dedication.

When summer arrived, I'd convince my father to take me to the Air Force swimming pool, specifically on days when I knew she might be there. Access to the pool was one of the privileges of military life, a recreational facility that compensated somewhat for the modest salaries and demanding work schedules.

At the tender age of seven, I would muster all my courage to dive from the deep end—a feat few of my peers attempted—secretly hoping she was watching my aquatic bravery. The diving board stood approximately one meter above the water's surface, but from my child's perspective, it might as well have been an aircraft carrier's flight deck. Climbing the short ladder, feeling the rough texture of the board beneath my feet, walking to the edge with deliberate steps that concealed my trembling knees, and finally launching myself into space—these moments represented a personal battle against fear, motivated by the possibility of impressing a girl who may or may not have even noticed.

My heart would pound not from physical exertion but from the proximity to my crush as I emerged from the water, casually (I thought) glancing in her direction to see if she had witnessed my feat of courage. Usually, she was completely absorbed in her own activities, oblivious to my aquatic displays of affection. On the rare occasions when our eyes did meet, I would immediately look away, my face burning hotter than the summer sun beating down on the pool deck.

That same romantic would spend the next decade secretly hoping to run into her again during our families' nomadic military postings across northern, western, and eastern India. Each new posting brought the tantalising possibility that her father might have been transferred to the same station, that I might turn a corner and suddenly encounter her in a new school corridor or at a base function. I would scan the faces of new classrooms with particular attention, hoping against hope for that familiar smile.

I remember the heartbreak at age eleven when her father was transferred to a northern Air Force base, creating a separation that felt insurmountable to my young heart. The news came through the efficient military grapevine—her father had received orders to move to Adampur, a fighter base in Punjab. The sight of their household items being loaded into a truck reinforced the impermanence that defined military childhoods—friendships, crushes, and connections all subject to the inexorable logic of service requirements and posting orders.

Spoiler alert: Despite traversing much of the subcontinent over the following ten years, landing up in Adampur within three years of being transferred there, I never did find her again. But, isn't that how the best childhood crushes go? First love, even at such a tender age, leaves an indelible mark on one's heart—a bittersweet memory that remains untarnished by reality, preserved in the amber of childhood innocence. In later years, I sometimes wondered what became of her—whether her father's career had continued in the Air Force, whether she had followed the typical pattern of military children and married into the services herself, whether she remembered the shy boy who dove from the high board hoping to catch her attention.

The beauty of such unresolved childhood attachments lies partly in their incompleteness—they remain perfect in memory precisely because they never evolved into the complicated reality of actual relationships. They exist in a perpetual state of possibility, untainted by arguments, disappointments, or the mundane realities that eventually temper adult relationships. My first crush remains forever seven years old in my memory, forever smiling, forever just slightly out of reach—a fitting metaphor, perhaps, for the ephemeral nature of Air Force childhoods themselves.

The Hidden Culture of Military Life

Life on an Air Force base came with its own peculiar highlights and rituals that civilians rarely witness—a hidden culture with unwritten rules and traditions that shaped my understanding of hierarchy, discipline, and community. To outsiders, military bases might appear as sterile, regimented environments where individuality is suppressed in favour of uniformity. The reality I experienced was far more nuanced and colourful, a world where strict protocols coexisted with deeply human moments and where formal hierarchies were occasionally suspended to allow for genuine connection.

I witnessed security guards who dined squatting on the floor of their mess, only using tables and chairs during annual inspections—a strange hierarchy that puzzled my young mind but introduced me to the complex social structures that existed even within military ranks. These guards, mostly from rural backgrounds, found comfort in traditional eating postures despite the Western-style furniture provided in their facilities. During routine days, the tables and chairs would be neatly arranged but unused, serving only as surfaces for storing items or displaying photographs of senior officers and national leaders. Only when senior officers conducted inspections would the furniture be employed for its intended purpose, creating a performance of modernity that satisfied official requirements while allowing personnel to maintain their cultural preferences in daily life.

I marvelled at wild Holi celebrations that terrified my young self, with colours flying and adults transformed into unrecognisable, jubilant revellers who seemed to abandon the strict decorum that usually governed military life temporarily. The festival of colours took on particular intensity at Air Force stations, where personnel who normally maintained careful distance by rank suddenly engaged in playful combat, smearing each other with vibrant powders and drenching one another with coloured water. Even the station commander wasn't exempt, often becoming a primary target for good-natured mischief from junior officers and airmen who would never dare approach him without proper salutes and deference on ordinary days.

My first Holi at Palam in 1976 remains etched in my memory—hiding behind my mother as a group of my father's colleagues approached our quarters, their faces already alienized by layers of purple, green, and red powders, carrying buckets of coloured water and packets of additional ammunition. Their laughter seemed almost maniacal to my four-year-old sensibilities, and I was convinced these strange creatures had nefarious intentions despite my parents' assurances that this was all in good fun. Eventually coaxed into participation, I discovered the liberating joy of temporarily abandoning cleanliness and order, though I remained a relatively conservative player compared to the adults who embraced the festival's chaotic spirit with abandon.

But nothing compared to the thrill of watching fighter jets roar overhead—Hunters from my father's "Flaming Arrows" squadron and the MiG-21s from the "Scorpions" squadron and TACDE (Tactics and Air Combat Development Establishment—India's equivalent of the US Navy's "Top Gun"). During every takeoff and landing, we waved frantically at pilots from our school playground near the runway. Our school's proximity to the airstrip meant that lunch breaks and games periods were frequently interrupted by the earth-shaking roar of aircraft taking off and landing, mixed with the distinct chop-chop of the helicopters. Especially the MiG-21s, the sleek, delta-winged interceptors capable of twice the speed of sound, created a distinctive shriek during takeoff that penetrated classroom walls and momentarily halted lessons as teachers paused, accustomed to these routine interruptions. At the same time, the Mi-4 helicopters announced their presence with the rhythmic thudding of rotor blades long before becoming visible.

Sometimes the low-flying helicopter pilots would wave back, creating an electric connection between earth and sky that made us feel special, chosen, and part of something greater than ourselves. These moments of acknowledgement—a gloved hand briefly raised in greeting visible from the cockpit's window—generated disproportionate excitement among us children. We would later debate whether the wave had been directed at a specific student or intended as a general greeting, claiming a personal connection to these aviators, who represented the pinnacle of military prestige and technical accomplishment.

"He waved directly at me!" I insisted after one such encounter, having positioned myself at the edge of the playground specifically to maximise my visibility.

"No way," my friend countered. "He was clearly waving at our whole class. Besides, he's my father's squadron mate—he knows me better than you!"

These good-natured arguments could continue for days, each child convinced of their special relationship with the pilots who soared above our ordinary lives. The possibility that these busy professionals might have simply been acknowledging the presence of children as a general courtesy never diminished our sense of personal connection to the aerial displays that punctuated our school days.

We imagine our fathers piloting those magnificent machines, although most were technicians and ground crew, inventing elaborate scenarios in which our dads performed heroic feats in the clouds above. My father, like most NCOs, worked in aircraft maintenance—his expertise focused on aircraft instrumentation rather than actual flying—but in my childhood imagination, I frequently promoted him to pilot status, mentally placing him in the cockpit of the aircraft he actually serviced from below. These fantasies reflected both pride in his actual contributions and a child's desire to associate his parents with the most glamorous role available in the immediate environment. The line between reality and imagination blurred easily in our young minds, allowing us to construct narratives that elevated our parents' roles within the military hierarchy. These innocent exaggerations were our way of claiming importance within a system where status was clearly defined by rank and role—a child's attempt to secure reflected glory from the machines that dominated our visual landscape.

These moments of pride were punctuated by the sobering reality of occasional crashes that reminded us of the dangers some of those men faced daily. When news of an accident spread through the base, a sombre mood would descend upon us children as we contemplated the violent, sudden nature of such deaths—early lessons in mortality that civilian children might be sheltered from until much later in life. The crash of a Hunter aircraft during my time at Jamnagar—an incident that claimed the life of a young Squadron Leader during a routine training sortie, while his wife was at the Air Force hospital expecting a baby—transformed our games for weeks afterwards. Our usual enthusiastic imitations of aircraft sounds and pretend dogfights temporarily ceased, replaced by more subdued activities and hushed discussions about what might have caused the accident and whether the pilot had suffered before the end.

During the funeral, the pilot's personal effects were packed by his colleagues and handed over to his wife, who had just delivered a baby girl the day he met his fate! For children observing these adult responses to tragedy, the message was clear: danger was real, sacrifice was possible, but the mission continued regardless of individual fate. This stoic approach to mortality would influence my understanding of risk and resilience throughout life, creating a perspective that acknowledged danger without being paralysed by it.

Technicolor Memories

Some memories stand out in technicolour, preserved with a vividness that belies the decades that have passed: fishing with bare hands in flooded streets after monsoon rains, feeling the slippery bodies of fish between my fingers as my younger brother and I laughed in the muddy water, our clothes ruined but our spirits soaring with the primitive joy of the catch. The monsoon transformed Jamnagar's landscape dramatically, converting dusty terrain into temporary waterways and creating opportunities for improvised childhood adventures that required no equipment beyond enthusiasm and parental inattention.

I remember how, after hefty downpours, the check dams around the city would overflow, sending fish swimming through streets transformed into temporary rivers. These fish—primarily small carp and catfish that inhabited the local reservoirs—found themselves suddenly displaced into urban environments, creating an unexpected bounty for opportunistic children. As the waters receded and collected in puddles, we children would wade into the muddy pools, using nothing but our hands to catch our slippery prizes—an activity that would have horrified our mothers had they known the full extent of our muddy adventures.

"Look! I got another one!" my two-year-old brother would shout, his small hands cupped around a wriggling silver fish no bigger than his palm. His face, splattered with mud but beaming with pride, reflected the simple joy of success in this primitive hunting method. We would proudly display our catches to each other, comparing sizes and species and making exaggerated claims about the difficulty of the capture, and presenting them to surprised parents as a potential contribution to the family dinner—an offering received with varying degrees of enthusiasm depending on the household's culinary flexibility.

Our mother, to her credit, would sometimes actually cook these muddy treasures, transforming them into simple fish curry that tasted like victory to us young hunters. More often, though, she would gently suggest that our catches might be "too small" or "need more time to grow," diplomatically redirecting our attention to the proper dinner she had already prepared. We were vaguely aware that our fishing expeditions existed in a grey area of parental approval—not explicitly forbidden but certainly not encouraged, particularly given the state of our clothing afterwards.

Then there was the magnificent Golden Jubilee air show in the autumn of 1982, featuring the "Thunderbolts" formation aerobatic display team in their Hunters, performing aerobatics that seemed to defy physics—loops, rolls, and precision formations that left spectators breathless and inspired a generation of children with the dream of flight. The celebration at Jamnagar featured a dazzling array of aircraft then in service with the Air Force—the British Hunters and Canberra bombers, the Soviet supersonic MiG-21 and MiG-23 fighters, and the Indian-made Marut fighters and Chetak helicopters. The Indian Air Force, established in 1932, was commemorating 50 years of service with demonstrations showcasing both its heritage and contemporary capabilities.

For weeks before the event, the base buzzed with preparations. Extra barracks were set up to accommodate visiting pilots and ground crews, rehearsals disrupted the usual flight schedules, and security measures intensified as the station prepared to welcome senior military officials and government dignitaries. For children, the most exciting development was the arrival of aircraft we had only seen in books or heard about in our fathers' stories, temporarily transforming our familiar base into an aviation circus.

The air show transformed the base into a temporary exhibition ground, with static displays of aircraft allowing the families rare close access to military hardware normally glimpsed only at a distance. I remember running from one display to another, marvelling at the Canberra bomber with its open bomb bay, the sleek Indian-made Marut fighters with their complement of rockets and bombs, and the Chetak helicopter decked out as a small elephant, complete with painted trunk and decorative blanket! Technical personnel stood beside each aircraft, patiently answering questions from the curious children and occasionally allowing us to climb the ladder for a peek into the cockpits under close supervision.

"Don't touch anything," my dad warned as he lifted me up to peer into the cockpit of a Hawker Hunter aircraft, "or you might accidentally eject yourself!" I froze immediately, my hands hovering inches from the controls until his chuckle revealed the joke. "The power's off, but still—hands in pockets, please." This brief glimpse into the pilot's domain, with its bewildering array of instruments and switches, only deepened my fascination with the machines that dominated our skyscape.

The aerial demonstrations, however, provided the most spectacular memories. The roar of engines, the gleaming metal fuselages catching sunlight, and the precision of the pilots created a spectacle that burned itself into my memory, reinforcing my fascination with flight and the men who commanded these powerful machines. The Thunderbolts' performance featured manoeuvres executed with such perfect synchronisation that the nine-aircraft formation appeared to function as a single entity—changing directions simultaneously, maintaining exact distances between wingtips during complex patterns, and creating geometric formations against the blue sky that elicited gasps and applause from the assembled crowd.

The solo aerobatic displays by the newly arrived MiG-23 proved equally impressive, with the pilot demonstrating manoeuvres that pushed both aircraft and human physiology to their limits. The barrel rolls, loops, inverted flights, and the ending with the "Vertical Charlie" manoeuvre (where the aircraft flies at a low altitude, pulls up sharply into a vertical climb, conducts multiple rolls, and disappears into the sky above) showcased not just technical flying skills but the physical conditioning required to withstand forces that compressed bodies during high-g turns and lifted them against restraining harnesses during negative-g manoeuvres. For children accustomed to considering physical education classes challenging, these demonstrations offered new perspectives on the demands of military aviation and the exceptional individuals who qualified for these roles.

I also recall my month-long feast of mutton curry twice daily during a jaundice-induced hospital stay at a naval station, where the white uniforms and morning drills contrasted sharply with the perpetual smell of sea salt that permeated everything. This unexpected circumstance introduced me to the distinctive culture of a different service branch, highlighting both similarities and differences in military medical practices.

The naval hospital presented an entirely different military culture — one where the rhythms of the sea rather than the sky dictated daily life, and where the crisp white uniforms seemed almost otherworldly compared to the familiar khaki of the Air Force. The naval personnel maintained traditions derived from the British Royal Navy, with terminology and protocols distinct from the more RAF demeanours (the British Royal Air Force traditions, which the IAF inherited) that I had grown accustomed to on Air Force bases. Doctors were addressed as "Surgeon Commander" rather than by the Air Force's medical ranks, and the daily routines incorporated nautical time designations and shipboard-derived procedures even within the landlocked hospital environment.

Despite my illness, I found the mutton curry so delicious that the hospital stay became associated with culinary pleasure rather than medical necessity in my memory — another example of how children find joy in unexpected circumstances. The naval hospital's kitchen, operating according to maritime traditions that recognised the importance of quality food for maintaining morale during extended deployments, produced meals superior to typical institutional fare. The mutton curry featured tender meat in a rich gravy seasoned with whole spices—cardamom, cinnamon, and cloves—that created an aromatic signature detectable throughout the ward during meal deliveries.

"You're eating better here than at home," my mother observed, both amused and slightly offended by my enthusiastic consumption of hospital food. I couldn't explain that it wasn't a reflection on her culinary skills but rather the novelty of these new flavours and the unexpected freedom of hospital life—where normal parental restrictions on television viewing and bedtime were temporarily suspended, creating a strange vacation-like atmosphere despite my jaundiced condition.

This culinary highlight transformed what might have been a miserable confinement into a period remembered primarily for gastronomic discovery, demonstrating children's remarkable ability to find silver linings in adverse situations. Years later, when I encountered similar spice combinations in restaurants, the aroma would instantly transport me back to that hospital ward—a connection between sensory experience and memory that preserved this childhood episode in vivid detail.

Festivals and Spiritual Dimensions

The annual Durga Puja celebrations at the Air Force camp were events we anticipated all year — an explosion of colour, devotion, and community that brought together military families from all backgrounds, ranks, and regions. These festivities created a temporary suspension of the usual hierarchies, allowing children like me to witness the rich cultural traditions that existed alongside military discipline. The Bengali community within the Air Force organised elaborate celebrations that attracted participation from personnel of various backgrounds, creating a pan-Indian cultural experience within the military environment.

Preparations would begin months in advance, with committees formed to handle logistics, fundraising, and artistic elements. The construction of the pandal—a temporary structure housing the Durga idol and associated decorations—became a community project involving off-duty personnel contributing labour according to their skills. Electricians created lighting arrangements that transformed simple materials into dazzling displays, carpenters built platforms and supports, and artists painted backdrops and designed ornamental elements. Children rehearsed cultural performances scheduled throughout the festival period, practising dance routines and dramatic presentations during evenings and weekends.

The arrival of the idol—made by one of the personnel at the station hailing from a traditional idol-maker family in Bengal—marked the official beginning of celebrations. The installation ceremony featured rituals performed by a priest specially brought in for the occasion, the officiating chairperson being the Air Officer Commanding (AOC) of the base. This juxtaposition of military authority with religious tradition created a fascinating blend of protocols—the AOC receiving both the formal salutes of his rank and the traditional offerings of flowers and sweets associated with the ceremony.

The subsequent days included morning prayers, afternoon cultural programmes, evening arati ceremonies with lamps and incense creating hypnotic patterns before the deity, and night-time performances ranging from classical music to contemporary film songs. The special attraction at Jamnagar was a movie show using a bioscope on the evening of the first day of the puja—a magical experience in which hand-cranked projectors displayed simple animations and film clips on a white sheet, creating cinema with the most basic technology. For children accustomed to watching movies only in proper theatres, this primitive projection method seemed almost miraculous, a fitting entertainment for a festival celebrating divine power.

For children, these festivals offered multiple attractions: special foods unavailable during ordinary times, extended social interactions with peers usually separated by school divisions or housing arrangements, freedom from usual bedtime restrictions, and opportunities to display talents in organised performances. The bhog distribution—free meals provided to all attendees as offerings first presented to the goddess—created memorable culinary experiences, with the distinctive khichuri (a preparation of rice and lentils with vegetables) developing associations with festive occasions rather than the simple comfort food it represented in other contexts.

Similarly, our family trips to Haridwar left me in awe as I watched the Ganga arati ceremonies, with flames leaping high after holy water was poured into large diyas, illuminating devotees' faces and creating dancing reflections on the sacred river. These pilgrimages, undertaken during leave periods when stationed at Palam near Delhi, introduced spiritual dimensions that complemented the technological environment of Air Force life. The journey itself—travelling from the structured, modernised military base to the ancient riverside city with its temples and ashrams—created a temporal transition that heightened awareness of India's continuous civilisation spanning millennia.

The evening arati ceremony at Har Ki Pauri ghat brought hundreds of devotees together along the riverbank, creating a community of worship that transcended the social categories operative in ordinary life. The priests performing the ceremony moved with choreographed precision, swinging large multi-tiered lamps in circular patterns that created trails of light against the darkening sky, while chants and bells created an acoustic environment that focused attention despite the large crowds.

I can still picture my father meditating peacefully on the banks of the Ganges while I watched, transfixed by his stillness amid the spiritual bustle. These moments revealed another dimension of my father—not just the Air Force serviceman but a spiritual seeker whose inner life contained depths I was only beginning to comprehend. The coexistence of military discipline and spiritual devotion in the same individual demonstrated an integration of seemingly disparate aspects of Indian identity—the modern technological state with its defence requirements alongside ancient religious traditions with their metaphysical concerns.

For a child growing up in the secular institutional environment of the Air Force, these religious excursions provided essential exposure to the cultural foundations that continued to inform Indian society despite modernisation efforts. The military, while officially non-sectarian and focused on national rather than religious identity, nevertheless accommodated and respected the spiritual practices of its personnel, recognising that these traditions formed part of the cultural heritage the armed forces existed to defend. This balanced approach, maintaining secular institutional structures while respecting religious expression, offered valuable lessons in how diverse traditions could coexist within a unified national framework.

Stories and Heritage

My father's storytelling shaped my imagination as much as the military shaped our lives. Lying beside him at night, in accommodations that often felt temporary but became home through these intimate rituals, I'd drift off to tales of ancient Indian epics—the Ramayana and Mahabharata—with their moral complexities, heroic characters, and divine interventions. These narratives, transmitted orally across generations, connected our modern military existence to cultural traditions thousands of years old, creating continuity between ancient values and contemporary service.

His voice would change subtly with each character—deepening for the noble Rama, taking on a mischievous lilt for the monkey-god Hanuman, becoming stern and righteous for Lord Krishna delivering the wisdom of the Bhagavad Gita. These vocal transformations transported me from our modest quarters to ancient battlefields and forest hermitages, creating mental images more vivid than any television programme could provide. The epic stories featured conflicts, strategies, and ethical dilemmas that paralleled military situations in abstract forms, offering frameworks for understanding concepts like duty, honour, and sacrifice that remained relevant despite technological transformations in warfare.

The Bhagavad Gita's central message—performing one's duty without attachment to results—resonated particularly with military service, where personnel must execute assigned responsibilities regardless of personal preferences or concerns about outcomes. My father would explain these philosophical concepts in simple terms appropriate for a child's understanding, planting seeds of ethical reasoning that would develop more fully as I matured. These bedtime philosophy sessions, disguised as entertainment, provided a moral compass that helped navigate the complexities of life within and beyond military environments.

He would also share stories of my grandfather and his compatriots who took part in the armed revolutionary movement against British colonial rule—tales of courage, sacrifice, and patriotism that connected me to a family legacy of service that predated the Air Force. My grandfather had participated in the underground resistance activities in Bengal during the 1920s and 1930s, risking imprisonment or worse to advance the cause of independence. Many of his fellow revolutionaries were either hanged or sent to Cellular Jail (Kala Pani). Grandfather was caught and spent twelve years in prisons all over erstwhile British India. These family histories reinforced in my tender mind the idea that defending the hard-won independence achieved by previous generations is a sacred trust that later generations must uphold.

The stories of my grandfather's imprisonment—the solidarity among political prisoners, the small acts of defiance against British authorities—created a personal connection to national history that textbooks alone could never achieve. I would imagine him in his cell, maintaining dignity despite harsh conditions, and feel both pride in his courage and gratitude that my own childhood unfolded in an independent India. These narratives planted seeds of patriotism and adventure in my young mind, reinforced by my experiences in Boy Scouts at age 10–11, where we marched long distances, learned to read maps and signs, and imagined ourselves as future defenders of our nation.

The scouting movement, with its emphasis on outdoor skills, self-reliance, and community service, complemented military values while operating in civilian contexts accessible to children. The structured activities—hiking expeditions, camp setups, and first-aid training—provided practical applications of concepts otherwise encountered only in stories or observed from a distance in adult military operations. The scout uniform became a source of pride, a precursor to the military uniform I imagined someday wearing, and the trekking expeditions offered a taste of the discipline and camaraderie that military service entails.

Wearing that uniform and participating in those long marches and picnics gave me my first taste of structured adventure—the thrill of exploration tempered by rules and protocols that ensured our safety and success. These early scouting experiences fostered both independence and teamwork, qualities that would serve me well throughout life. The seemingly contradictory emphasis on both individual capability and group coordination mirrored military approaches that required each person to develop specific skills while functioning within a larger unit with collective objectives.

Heroes in Print and Reality

By day, I devoured comics featuring Phantom and Flash Gordon, eagerly awaiting new Indrajal comics each week, scanning the local book shop at the air force station for the latest issues that would transport me to worlds of adventure and heroism. The weekly hunt for new comics became a ritual that punctuated the rhythm of my childhood—each new issue a portal to worlds where justice prevailed and heroes triumphed against impossible odds.

The Phantom particularly captured my imagination—a hero who relied on intelligence and physical training rather than supernatural powers, who lived in the mysterious African jungle but travelled worldwide to fight evil, who passed his mantle down through generations, creating the illusion of immortality. His combination of mystery, moral clarity, and global adventures resonated with my military-influenced sensibilities, offering a model of heroism that seemed potentially achievable through discipline and dedication rather than alien origins or radioactive accidents.

These Western superheroes shared space in my imagination with the historical and mythological figures from Amar Chitra Katha comics, which transported me to India's warrior past, allowing me to imagine myself as a hero from another time—perhaps a brave Rajput warrior or a freedom fighter sacrificing everything for independence. The colourful illustrations and dramatic narratives of these comics provided accessible entry points to complex historical and mythological traditions, creating emotional connections to cultural heritage that formal education often failed to inspire.

This blend of Western and Indian heroic traditions created a rich internal landscape where courage, honour, and justice were paramount values—values that aligned perfectly with the military ethos surrounding me. Through these illustrated pages, I developed not just a love of storytelling but also an appreciation for different cultural perspectives on heroism and virtue—Western individualism alongside Indian concepts of dharma and collective duty.

Cross-Country Journeys

The annual visit to my grandparents' home in eastern India—a three-day train journey across the subcontinent—was a sensory explosion that educated me more profoundly than any classroom could. These epic journeys, undertaken in the crowded compartments of Indian Railways, became a yearly education in geography, sociology, and cultural diversity. The changing landscapes, languages, foods, and aromas created a moving tapestry of India that no textbook could capture.

From the western states of Gujarat and Maharashtra, with their distinct cuisines and dialects, through the heart of central India with its rugged terrain and tribal influences, across the Gangetic plains of Bihar with their agricultural bounty and historical significance, and finally to West Bengal with its literary heritage and revolutionary history—each mile revealed a new facet of my country's diversity. The train windows framed an ever-changing portrait of India: farmers tending fields, children playing cricket in village clearings, women in colourful saris carrying water, and ancient temples standing alongside modern ones.

Reflections on Early Childhood Years

Looking back on those formative years under the shadow of wings, I realise how profoundly my Air Force childhood shaped me. The constant relocations taught me adaptability, while the structured military environment instilled discipline that remains with me today. My early adventures—from diving boards to flooded streets—weren't just childhood escapades but lessons in courage and resilience. The contrast between technological might and spiritual tradition created a worldview that embraces both modernity and heritage.

Most precious were those moments of connection: my father's bedtime stories linking ancient wisdom to contemporary challenges; the electric thrill when helicopter pilots acknowledged our existence with a simple wave; the community bonds forged during festivals that transcended rank and region. Even my unrequited first crush taught me about impermanence and the beauty of possibilities left unexplored.

In these memories of an Air Force childhood, I find the foundations of who I've become—someone who learned to find home in motion and stability in stories. The constant movement taught resilience; the exposure to diverse regions of India fostered both patriotism and cultural appreciation; the military environment instilled discipline, while the freedom of childhood nurtured imagination. The tension between these forces—structure and freedom, permanence and change, individual and community—created a unique crucible for identity formation. I am, in many ways, still chasing horizons—still the child who learned to find home in motion, stability in stories, and belonging in the vast, varied tapestry of experiences that constituted life as an Air Force brat in mid- to late-1970s and early-1980s India.

Chapter 2

Shadows of Conflict: Coming of Age in Punjab's Troubled Skies

Prelude to Turbulence

They say childhood ends gradually, but mine concluded with the distinct sound of gunfire. Looking back, I can pinpoint the exact moments when my carefree Air Force childhood began its transformation into something more complex. It started with a series of incidents at Jamnagar in 1983 that, at the time, seemed merely interesting disruptions to our routine but were actually foreshadowing the turbulent experiences awaiting me in Punjab.

I was twelve years old, still collecting *Phantom* comics and playing cricket with friends, when two MiG-21 fighters returned to Jamnagar base after range-firing sorties. One aircraft had a bomb that had misfired and was still hanging precariously from the undercarriage. Word spread quickly through the base housing, and soon all the children were buzzing with nervous excitement.

"My dad says it could fall off and explode any minute," one of my friends announced with the peculiar blend of terror and thrill that only pre-teens can muster when discussing potential disasters.

"No way," another countered. "They have special safety mechanisms."

"My father says they're going to try to remove it tonight," a third chimed in, eager to contribute insider information gleaned from overheard adult conversations.

I remained silent, watching the adults' faces for clues. Despite their practised military composure, I could detect the tension in their eyes, the way conversations would halt when children approached, the subtle increase in the pace of their movements. It was like watching actors who knew their audience could see behind the curtain but were determined to maintain the performance anyway.

For two days, this suspended anxiety hung over the base like the monsoon clouds that gathered but never broke. The technical staff worked around the clock, consulting manuals and experts, developing a plan to remove the volatile ordnance safely. Then, one evening, an earth-shattering boom shook our quarters, rattling windows and knocking a framed photograph off our wall. Massive plumes of smoke rose in the distance, visible even from our location several kilometres away. The technical staff had carefully removed the volatile ordnance and transported it to a safe area for controlled detonation. The explosion, even from a distance, was unlike anything I had experienced—a physical force that seemed to compress the air in my lungs before releasing it, a tangible demonstration of the destructive power contained in the sleek machines I had admired since childhood.

"That was just one bomb," my father explained later, his voice unusually solemn as we watched the smoke dissipate in the evening sky. "Imagine what a full payload could do." He did not need to imagine—having experienced being strafed and rocketed by Pakistan Air Force F-86 Sabre jets and F-104 Starfighters during daytime air raids and bombed by B-57 bombers during nighttime raids at Halwara air base, where he served with the Battle-Axes squadron during the 1965 Indo-Pak war. He described how fighter aircraft like the MiG-21 could carry multiple bombs, rockets, and missiles, each with a destructive capacity far exceeding what we had just witnessed. It was my first lesson in the reality behind the aerial ballets I had watched with such fascination—these weren't just magnificent flying machines but instruments of destruction, their beauty inseparable from their deadly purpose.

This sobering realisation was reinforced shortly afterwards when a blast occurred in the bomb dump on the base—an accident that claimed the lives of some airmen. The whispered conversations among adults grew hushed when we children approached, but fragments reached our ears nonetheless: only lumps of flesh had been recovered for the funeral ceremonies. The abstract concept of military danger suddenly became concrete, leaving an impression that no safety briefing or cautionary tale could have conveyed.

The final ominous development at Jamnagar came when two Sten machine carbines went missing from the armoury. Security measures intensified overnight—additional guards appeared at checkpoints, identity verification became more thorough, and personnel were advised to report any suspicious activities immediately. We heard rumours that these weapons were linked to Khalistani terrorists, but at age twelve, I didn't fully comprehend what this meant. The term "Khalistani" floated through adult conversations like an unfamiliar spectre, creating tension without context. I couldn't have known then how intimately acquainted I would soon become with this movement and its consequences.

"What's a Khalistani?" I asked my father one evening after overhearing a particularly intense discussion among his colleagues.

He hesitated, clearly weighing how much to explain to a twelve-year-old. "They're people who want to create a separate country called Khalistan for Sikhs," he finally said. "They believe Sikhs aren't treated fairly in India."

"But we have Sikh neighbours," I protested, thinking of the kind family next door who always shared sweets during festivals. "They seem happy here."

"Most Sikhs are loyal Indians," he agreed. "But some extremists are using violence to push for separation. It's complicated, Baba. Sometimes good people get caught between different ideas of what's right."

This explanation, while simplified for my understanding, introduced concepts of political identity and separatism that would soon become painfully relevant to our daily lives. The missing weapons, which were recovered later, were part of a larger pattern of arms theft that fuelled the growing insurgency in Punjab—a conflict that would soon engulf our new home.

Transition to Amritsar

Father was transferred to an Air NCC (National Cadet Corps) unit at Amritsar in late 1983. Despite the unsettling incidents at Jamnagar, we were excited about the move. Six years at one station was unusually long for military families, and the prospect of new surroundings appealed to our nomadic instincts. The familiar ritual of packing commenced—wooden boxes (which were actually repurposed bomb crates, their previous purpose evident in the stencilled warnings partially visible beneath new labels) filled with our modest possessions.

These crates had their own history, having once contained actual ordnance before being repurposed for domestic use—a common practice in the resource-conscious military environment. The irony wasn't lost on me even then: containers designed for instruments of destruction now protecting our family photographs, kitchen utensils, and my precious comic book collection. My mother would line them with newspapers before carefully arranging our belongings, transforming military surplus into civilian necessity with practised efficiency.

The logistics of military transfers revealed the economic realities of service life. The Air Force didn't provide sufficient allowances to cover the full cost of transporting a family's belongings, so airmen resorted to creative solutions. I remember discussions about offering rum bottles from the service canteen to the railway clerks to convince them to allow our extra luggage without additional charges. These minor corruptions were treated as necessary compromises in a system that demanded mobility without adequately funding it.

"It's not a bribe," my father explained when he noticed my confused expression during one such conversation with a colleague. "It's a token of appreciation for their flexibility." He went on to describe how railway regulations technically limited the amount of luggage each passenger could carry, but clerks had discretion to overlook minor excesses. The rum—available at subsidised rates in military canteens—served as an unofficial currency that facilitated these transactions without direct monetary exchange.

This distinction, while perhaps lost on my twelve-year-old self, introduced me to the grey areas of adult morality—how principles sometimes bend under practical necessities without quite breaking. It was another lesson in the complex reality behind official systems and regulations, where informal practices often filled gaps left by institutional limitations. These unofficial arrangements, I would later understand, were part of the invisible infrastructure that made military life functional despite bureaucratic constraints.

We travelled through Delhi on our way to Amritsar. During a several-hour break between trains, we visited the Red Fort, where I purchased a toy that captured my imagination—a catapult-fired parachute. The simple device consisted of a plastic paratrooper figure attached to a folded parachute, which could be launched skyward using a rubber-band catapult. I was endlessly amused watching the folded parachute being launched skyward, then deploying as the plastic toy paratrooper drifted slowly back to earth. In my mind, I was that paratrooper, dropping behind enemy lines on some crucial mission. The irony that I would soon be living in what amounted to a conflict zone was lost on me at the time.

"Look how high it goes!" I exclaimed to my brother after a particularly successful launch that sent the paratrooper soaring above the tourists milling around the historic fort. "I bet real paratroopers feel just like this when they jump!"

My father smiled at my enthusiasm but added a gentle reality check: "Real paratroopers carry heavy equipment and often jump at night into dangerous situations. It's not quite as fun as your toy makes it look." This was typical of his parenting approach—encouraging imagination while subtly introducing the complexities of the real military operations that my toys simplified and romanticised.

When we finally reached Amritsar, the December cold of North India hit us with shocking intensity. Having spent six years in coastal Jamnagar, we were unprepared for the biting winter of the Punjab plains. The temperature difference was dramatic—from Jamnagar's mild winter lows of perhaps 25°C (77°F) to Amritsar's frigid 2°C (35°F), occasionally dropping below freezing at night. Our wardrobe, adapted to Gujarat's coastal climate, proved woefully inadequate for this northern chill.

I didn't even own full-length trousers for my school uniform and initially wore black pants instead of the required navy blue, a minor uniform infraction that highlighted our family's perpetual state of adaptation to new circumstances. The black pants, hastily purchased from a local market as a stopgap measure, were slightly too short and made of a material that offered little protection against the cold morning air.

"You look like you're going to a funeral, not school," my mother observed with a mix of amusement and concern as she surveyed my makeshift uniform on the first day. She promised to purchase proper navy trousers as soon as possible, but in the meantime, I would have to face the scrutiny of teachers and classmates in my improvised attire.

"Maybe they won't notice," I suggested hopefully, though we both knew this was unlikely. School authorities in military environments were particularly strict about uniform compliance, viewing it as part of the discipline that prepared children for potential future service.

"Just explain that we've newly arrived from Jamnagar," she advised practically. "Most teachers understand the challenges of transfer postings." Her confidence proved justified; my teacher accepted the explanation with a nod, though she did note that a proper uniform would be expected within the week.

Our first night in Amritsar brought an earthquake, a literal tremor that seemed, in retrospect, a fitting metaphor for the social and political upheaval we were about to experience. The shaking woke us from sleep, causing momentary panic as we tried to orient ourselves in an unfamiliar house in the darkness. My father, ever calm in emergencies, guided us to stand in doorways until the trembling subsided, then checked the structure for any damage before allowing us to return to bed.

"The earth is just welcoming us to Punjab," he joked, trying to ease our tension. "A little shake to make sure we're paying attention." His ability to find humour in unsettling situations was a quality I would come to appreciate even more in the turbulent months ahead.

We quickly settled into our new surroundings, making friends and establishing routines. Although father was posted to the NCC unit, Amritsar had an Air Force long-range radar unit with separate accommodation for staff. We didn't qualify for quarters on the base but secured a small civil accommodation adjacent to the Air Force camp and directly opposite the "Panther" officers' mess (named for the "Panther" Infantry Division based at

Amritsar). This proximity to military facilities would later prove providential in ways we couldn't have anticipated.

Our house was modest but comfortable, one room and a kitchen, an open bathroom with a shared toilet for the landlord and two tenants, including us. The walls were whitewashed and bare when we arrived, but my mother quickly transformed the space with familiar objects: framed family photographs, a calendar featuring Hindu deities, colourful cushion covers she had embroidered herself. These personal touches created continuity amid change, making each new posting feel like home despite the different physical structures.

I formed friendships with other Bengali children at the Air Force station, creating a small gang united by shared cultural background and the universal experience of being military dependents. We navigated the new school environment together, finding comfort in our collective identity as outsiders who understood each other's nomadic lifestyles.

"You're from Jamnagar? We were there three years ago!" a boy exclaimed during our first meeting, immediately establishing the connection that military children form through shared geographies if not shared timelines. "Did you know Squadron Leader Mukherjee's elder son? He was my best friend before they moved to Pathankot."

I knew the younger son, who was my classmate in the 2nd standard and got more attention from my lady love at school in Jamnagar. With a tinge of forgotten ache somewhere deep within, I let it pass. The mere possibility of overlapping connections was enough to establish camaraderie with new friends. Within days, we were trading comics, sharing tiffin lunches and planning weekend adventures as though we'd known each other for years rather than days, another example of the accelerated intimacy that military children develop out of necessity.

Our conversations often centred on comparing our various postings: which base had the best cinema, which school was the strictest, which mess served the best food during special functions. These discussions served multiple purposes: establishing our credentials as experienced military brats, sharing practical information about navigating different stations and creating a shared narrative that validated our unusual lifestyle.

"Jamnagar has the best swimming pool," I would assert confidently.

"Maybe, but Hindon has better movies," another would counter.

"You're both wrong, nothing beats the ice cream at Agra Air Force Station," a third would declare, launching us into good-natured debates that could continue for hours.

These friendships provided essential stability during a period when the larger environment was becoming increasingly unstable. As we compared notes on different Air Force stations and swapped stories about our fathers' various postings, we were also unconsciously reinforcing our identity as military children, distinct from the civilian population around us and united by experiences that outsiders couldn't fully comprehend.

Gathering Clouds

As the academic session concluded in the summer of 1984, we looked forward to holidays filled with comics, games, and the carefree activities that defined childhood summers. However, an undercurrent of tension was becoming increasingly difficult to ignore. The Khalistani separatist movement was gaining momentum throughout Punjab, with incidents of violence becoming more frequent and brazen.

The signs were subtle at first: increased security checks at the base entrance, adults speaking in hushed tones when discussing news reports, casual outings to the city becoming less frequent and more carefully planned. Then came more obvious indicators: armed guards appearing at public buildings, police patrols becoming more visible in civilian areas, and occasional distant sounds of disturbances that adults would dismiss as "nothing to worry about" with unconvincing casualness.

One particularly disturbing event penetrated even our childish bubble of security: a BSF (Border Security Force) school transport was hijacked by terrorists. They released most of the children but took the son of the BSF commandant hostage. Although the boy was eventually released after negotiations, the incident terrified parents throughout the military community. The targeting of children—specifically a child chosen for his father's position—introduced a new dimension of vulnerability that affected how we were allowed to move about and play.

"Stay within sight of the quarters," my mother instructed, her usual relaxed attitude toward our wanderings suddenly replaced by vigilance. "And come immediately when called—no excuses about 'five more minutes' of football."

The freedom we had previously enjoyed, roaming the neighbourhood until dusk, visiting friends in nearby quarters without specific permission, cycling to the base canteen for occasional treats, was gradually curtailed. Parents began coordinating supervision schedules to ensure that children were always under adult supervision. Spontaneous play was replaced by organised activities within secure areas. The carefree summer we had anticipated was transforming into something more restricted and anxious.

We also heard reports from around Punjab of terrorists singling out Hindu passengers from buses and executing them. These sectarian killings confused and troubled me deeply. Punjab had a long tradition of religious integration; many Hindu families would traditionally "give" their eldest son to the Khalsa, making him an "Amrit Dhari" Sikh. This practice created a literal brotherhood between the communities, with Sikhs and Hindus often being siblings born to the same parents. How could a brother kill his brother in the name of some imagined religious injustice? This question troubled me far more than any fear for my personal safety.

"But Sikhs and Hindus are family," I protested when my father explained why we needed to be more cautious when travelling. "How can they hurt each other?"

"Most don't want to," he explained carefully. "But extremists are trying to create division. They want Sikhs and Hindus to see each other as enemies instead of brothers. That's why violence against innocent people is their weapon; it creates fear and anger that separates communities that have lived together for centuries."

This explanation made intellectual sense but remained emotionally incomprehensible to me. In my limited experience, religious identity had been a matter of interesting differences in customs and celebrations, not a reason for hatred or violence. The idea that someone might kill another person based solely on which house of worship they attended seemed both irrational and terrifying, a violation of the basic humanity I had been taught to recognise in everyone.

Despite these gathering clouds, May 1984 provided one of the most unforgettable and joyful memories of my childhood. Our exams were over, and Dad took my brother and me to the flying club at Raja Sansi Airport. I was twelve and my brother eight, both of us excited about visiting the facility where Air NCC cadets received basic flight training.

The flying club was a modest operation with a small hangar, located at one corner of a larger airport used by civilian airlines but also acting as an emergency forward air base for the Indian Air Force. A few light aircraft, including the Indian-built Pushpak microlight, were parked near the hangar for basic flight instruction.

We watched a Pushpak microlight aircraft land and taxi toward the hangar where we were waiting. The plane stopped nearby but kept its engine running, its propeller creating a visible disc in the bright morning sunlight. When the trainee pilot disembarked, the instructor remained in the cockpit and waved for us to approach. To our astonishment, he gestured for us to climb aboard. Unknown to us, our father had arranged permission for us to experience a brief flight—a surprise that sent our excitement levels soaring.

"Really? We're going to fly?" my brother squealed, bouncing on his toes with barely contained enthusiasm.

My father nodded, smiling at our reaction. "Just a short flight around the pattern," he confirmed. "The instructor is a friend who agreed to take you up. Remember to thank him properly afterwards."

The anticipation was overwhelming as we squeezed into the trainee's side of the cockpit, my brother and I sharing the single seat designed for one adult. The space was cramped, but we were too excited to complain, our bodies pressed together as we buckled the single safety belt around both our waists. The cockpit smelled of aviation fuel, leather, and the indefinable scent of machinery—an aroma I would forever associate with the thrill of flight.

We were strictly instructed not to touch anything—not the control yoke that protruded from the instrument panel, not the rudder pedals beneath our dangling feet, not any of the gauges and switches that covered the dashboard. My brother gripped my hand tightly, and I returned the pressure, both of us vibrating with nervous energy. In our excitement, we forgot to close the glass window after the door was shut—an oversight my brother would later blame for the wind blast that partially obscured his view during the flight.

"Ready, boys?" the instructor asked, his voice barely audible over the engine noise and our pounding hearts.

We nodded vigorously, too thrilled to speak. The aircraft began rolling down the runway, gradually gathering speed. The bumpy concrete surface transmitted every irregularity to the airframe, creating a vibration that seemed to penetrate our bones. Then the nose lifted slightly, the bumping sensation ceased abruptly, and a strange weightlessness took its place. The transition from ground to air happened so smoothly that I wasn't immediately aware we had left terra firma. The realisation came when I looked down and saw several abandoned old fighters (old Su-7 fighter jets used as decoys) within the airport perimeter, suddenly appearing toy-like below us.

"We're flying!" my brother shouted unnecessarily, his voice high with excitement. "We're actually flying!"

When the aircraft banked left, we experienced a horrifying sensation of falling, causing us to grip each other even more tightly. My brother let out a small yelp that he would later vehemently deny. The instructor glanced over with a reassuring smile, clearly accustomed to first-time flyers' reactions to banking manoeuvres. As the plane straightened out, the pilot pointed out tiny houses, buffalo roaming on farms, and vehicles on roads that looked like miniature toys. The perspective was utterly surreal—the familiar landscape of our daily lives transformed into a living map.

"That's a Gurudwara!" I shouted, spotting the distinctive dome with a golden spire.

The flight continued for perhaps fifteen minutes, though it felt both longer and shorter—time seemed to expand with the intensity of new sensations while simultaneously accelerating with excitement. After a few more banks and turns, I saw the runway approaching and knew our dream experience was ending. The touchdown felt slightly jerky, but I was still processing the sensation of flight when the aircraft came to a stop. We unbuckled and stepped back onto the tarmac, forever changed by those brief minutes in the air. I've flown so many times in the last three decades in big commercial airliners, including in lavish business-class ambience, but nothing came remotely close to flying in the cramped cockpit of that microlight aircraft in the summer of 1984.

For two children who had grown up watching fighter jets take to the skies, we experienced firsthand the meaning of the Indian Air Force motto: "Nabhaha Sparsham Deeptam" (touching the sky with glory).

"So?" our father asked as we rejoined him, his face betraying the pleasure he took in our evident excitement.

"It was AMAZING!" my brother shouted, his earlier fear completely forgotten. "Can we go again tomorrow?"

Dad laughed. "Let's not push our luck. Some experiences are special precisely because they don't happen every day."

I was quieter, still processing the strange sensation of having seen the world from above—how it simultaneously expanded my perspective and made everything seem more minor. It was a metaphor I would revisit many times in later years, particularly when trying to make sense of the conflicts that human beings create over what, from above, appear to be arbitrary divisions on a continuous landscape.

"Thank you," I finally said to both my father and the instructor, trying to convey the depth of my gratitude for an experience I knew I would remember forever.

"You're welcome," the instructor replied with a smile. "Maybe someday you'll be flying these machines yourself."

I nodded, though I knew even then that my poor eyesight would likely disqualify me from a pilot's career. Still, the experience had connected me more deeply to the aviation environment that had always surrounded me, transforming me from mere observer to participant, however briefly.

As we drove home, the contrast between the transcendent joy of flight and the troubled ground reality of Punjab created a cognitive dissonance that I couldn't articulate but deeply felt. How could a place that offered such sublime experiences also harbour such darkness? This paradox—the coexistence of beauty and danger, freedom and constraint, joy and sorrow—would become increasingly apparent in the weeks ahead.

Operation Bluestar

Soon after this high point, our father left for what was supposed to be a week-long assignment, taking NCC cadets to a trekking camp at Dehradun–Mussoorie. That week would stretch into a month due to circumstances none of us could have predicted, leaving my mother to navigate the coming crisis alone with two children in an unfamiliar city.

The day after his departure usually began the same: school, homework, and the ritualistic evening games with neighbourhood friends. But subtle signs of something unusual were apparent to those paying attention. Military vehicles moved more frequently on nearby roads. Local shopkeepers seemed tense, closing earlier than usual. Neighbours spoke in hushed tones, their conversations ceasing when children approached.

When my father's colleagues returned after seeing him off at the railway station, they spoke in hushed tones about the heavy military presence they had observed in the city. "Soldiers everywhere," another added. "Something big is coming." They advised my mother to stock essential supplies—food, water, medicines—without explaining exactly why.

That evening, we witnessed an unprecedented movement of military convoys passing our home. Truck after truck loaded with soldiers, jeeps mounted with machine guns—all moving toward the city centre with grim purpose. More alarming was the sight of an infantry company from the Bihar Regiment taking up defensive positions in a guava orchard behind our houses. Soldiers dug shallow trenches, positioned LMGs (light machine guns), and established observation posts among the fruit trees where we had played just days earlier.

"Why are the soldiers in our orchard?" my brother asked innocently as we watched from our back window.

"They're just exercising," my mother replied, her forced casualness fooling neither of us. "Let's stay inside today and play carrom instead of going out."

Something significant was clearly imminent, though we children could only speculate about what it might be. My friends and I exchanged theories ranging from war with Pakistan to preparation for a visiting dignitary, none of us grasping the actual situation developing around us.

The answer came one night when the world suddenly seemed to explode around us. Shortly after midnight, we were awakened by sounds that I had previously heard only in war movies. The air filled with the staccato rhythm of machine-gun fire, the distinctive "swoosh" of rocket-propelled grenades, and the percussion of detonating grenades and shells, punctuated by the booms of artillery guns and tank fire. Operation Bluestar—the Indian Army's assault on the Golden Temple complex to flush out Khalistani terrorists led by Jarnail Singh Bhindranwale—had begun.

My brother crawled into my bed that night, his small body trembling with each explosion. I put my arm around him, pretending a confidence I didn't feel.

"It's okay," I whispered. "The Army is just getting rid of bad guys."

"But it's so loud," he whimpered. "What if they come here?"

"They won't," I assured him, though I had no basis for this certainty. "Dad's friends will protect us." I was referring to the Air Force personnel stationed nearby, though I had no idea whether they were involved in the operation or what they could do if the fighting spread to our area.

Sleep was nearly impossible with the constant noise of combat, but eventually exhaustion overcame fear, and we drifted into uneasy slumber, startling awake at particularly loud explosions. Morning brought no relief — the fighting continued unabated, and now we could see smoke rising from the direction of the Golden Temple.

The operation continued for several days, creating a surreal experience in which we watched sanitised news reports on television while hearing the sounds of battle in real time through our windows. The disconnect between official narratives and our lived reality was stark: while announcers spoke of "surgical operations" and "minimal force," we heard the unmistakable sounds of heavy weaponry and sustained combat.

A statewide curfew was imposed across Punjab, severely restricting movement and disrupting the supply of essential items such as food and milk. Our proximity to Air Force and Army camps proved advantageous, ensuring access to necessities, though the vegetables were often less than fresh—a minor inconvenience compared to the hardships faced by civilian families who lacked such connections.

"We're lucky," my mother reminded us when we complained about eating the same dal for the third day in a row. "Many people have nothing to eat right now." Her perspective check silenced our grumbling, instilling an early appreciation for our relative privilege even under challenging circumstances.

What we didn't initially realise was that the battle wasn't confined to the Golden Temple complex. The reason for the infantry company's position in the orchard behind our homes became clear on the second day of Operation Bluestar, when militants in Gumatala, a village visible from our house across another road, opened fire with automatic weapons and RPGs (rocket-propelled grenades).

The soldiers ordered us to remain indoors as the firefight intensified. From partially opened windows, we watched in a mixture of terror and fascination as bullets and rocket-propelled grenades whizzed overhead. Soldiers crawled across the melting pitch of the road in the peak summer heat, attempting to outflank the militants under cover of their own LMG (light machine gun) fire. The engagement concluded by evening with all the terrorists killed and the Army securing the village.

This proximity to actual combat—not a distant historical event or a scene in a movie but a life-and-death struggle unfolding before our eyes—created an indelible impression. The sounds, smells, and sights of battle became viscerally real: the distinctive odour of cordite that hung in the air afterwards, the brass shell casings that littered the road the next day, the bullet holes in walls and trees that remained as mute testimony to the violence.

Throughout this period, we observed a grim pattern in the military traffic passing our house on Ajnala Road from the Golden Temple complex to Raja Sansi airport. In the mornings, convoys full of troops would travel from the airport (where they arrived on Air Force transport planes) toward the operation zones. In the late afternoons and evenings, return convoys carried noticeably fewer soldiers back to the airport. Initially, we wondered about the discrepancy in numbers, not comprehending the human cost of the operation.

Understanding came at night when darkened, covered Army trucks moved silently from the operation sites to the airport. Even with their canvas covers and the drivers' attempts at discretion, we could hear muffled cries of pain from wounded and dying soldiers. The abstract concept of casualties became concrete in those moments—these weren't statistics but men suffering real pain, men who had families like ours waiting for them somewhere.

"Why are they crying?" my brother asked one night as a particularly vocal wounded soldier passed by our window.

I struggled to find an appropriate explanation for an eight-year-old. "They're hurt," I finally said. "They're brave soldiers who got injured fighting the bad guys."

"Will they get better?"

I wanted to say yes, to reassure him that good always triumphs and heroes always recover, but the raw sounds of agony suggested otherwise. "Some will," I answered honestly. "But fighting for what's right sometimes means getting hurt."

This exchange, simple as it was, marked a significant moment in my own understanding of conflict. The heroic narratives of war that had filled my comics and action figures were colliding with the messy, painful reality of actual combat. There were no clean victories, no unscathed heroes—just human beings suffering for causes they might not fully understand but were duty-bound to serve.

By late June, the situation was sufficiently under control for transportation restrictions to be lifted, allowing our father to return after his unexpected month-long absence. His reunion with us was emotional—he had spent weeks not knowing exactly what dangers we might be facing, receiving only sporadic updates through military channels. The relief on his face when he found us safe was palpable, though he quickly resumed his usual composed demeanour.

"You've all been courageous," he told us, embracing each family member in turn. "I'm proud of how you handled yourselves." This simple acknowledgement of our endurance meant more than elaborate praise might have—it recognised that we, too, had served in our way by maintaining stability in his absence during a crisis.

Our school, located in the cantonment, reopened in mid-July rather than early June because the building had been repurposed to house approximately 1,000 prisoners apprehended during Operation Bluestar. When we finally returned to classes, the school grounds were overgrown with tall grass, and we spent our games periods cutting it instead of playing sports. The school building itself showed subtle signs of its temporary conversion to a detention facility—reinforced locks on classroom doors, windows secured with additional bars, and strange markings on walls that no one would explain.

The relatively new school building had been fitted with a public address system that allowed for "indoor" morning assemblies during the monsoon season. Instructions, prayers, and the national anthem were broadcast throughout the building—an arrangement we found novel and slightly amusing, having never experienced morning assembly conducted over loudspeakers before.

"Attention!" the principal's voice would boom through the corridors, startling us despite our expectation of the announcement. "Stand for the national anthem!" And then the familiar strains of *Jana Gana Mana* would echo through the building, creating a strange, disconnected feeling as we stood at attention in our separate classrooms, united by sound but unable to see the flag or each other.

This technological solution to a practical problem—conducting assembly during monsoon rains—seemed particularly appropriate in the aftermath of Operation Bluestar. Like the sanitised news reports that had described the conflict without capturing its reality, the disembodied voice and music created a simulation of unity and normalcy that masked the fractures beneath. We performed the rituals of school life while carrying within us experiences that had fundamentally changed our understanding of the world.

Adampur: New Posting, New Tensions

Our stay in Amritsar lasted only eight months. Father was promoted to the rank of Junior Warrant Officer and posted to a maintenance flight (sub-unit) of a MiG-21 squadron, which shared the maintenance infrastructure of another MiG-21 squadron, the "Hawkeyes," at Adampur (the leading squadron of my dad's unit—the "Falcons"—was at Sirsa). Adampur air base also housed two newly raised MiG-23 air-defence fighter squadrons (the "Tridents" and the "Warlords" squadrons). We relocated in August 1984, during the peak of the monsoon season. I vividly remember the torrential rain when we reached Jalandhar Cantt Railway Station from Amritsar, having experienced downpours throughout our two-hour train journey.

We managed to unload all our luggage during the brief two-minute halt and transferred it to the Air Force posting run—the ubiquitous three-tonner "Shaktiman" truck that transported us to

Khurdpur village near Adampur air base. Our new accommodation was modest civil housing, with the most shocking feature being the open toilet on the roof. It consisted of just two bricks to squat on, with waste remaining exposed all day until being cleaned by the village sanitation worker before dawn the following morning—a stark contrast to the facilities we had grown accustomed to on Air Force bases.

School life at Adampur presented new adventures. As a 13-year-old "young man," I walked daily to school from our village home along an almost deserted road lined with enormous eucalyptus trees. The route took me past an irrigation canal, sugarcane fields, an unmanned railway crossing, a small church near the air base habitation, and finally the Air Force guard room before reaching the school, which was situated near both the guard post and a small Air Force cinema theatre.

Winter mornings transformed this journey into something magical. Low-hanging fog created an ethereal landscape, and strange spider-web patterns appeared on the grass alongside the path. One day, after forgetting to bring in a pillow we had left on the roof to sun, we discovered it covered with a thin layer of ice the next morning—the dew had frozen in the notorious winter chill of North India. This made me realise that the mysterious "spider webs" on the grass during my morning walks were actually frozen dew. I was thrilled to know that I was literally "walking on thin ice" every day to school!

The experience was less enchanting for my younger brother, only eight years old at the time. He had to rise before dawn during those cold winter mornings to catch the early school transport—another Shaktiman truck—to attend Vajra Army School at Jalandhar Cantt (named after the "Vajra" Corps—comprising three infantry divisions and other support elements, headquartered there). He would return after dark, his days entirely consumed by the demands of education and transportation.

Our school at Adampur was a fascinating extension of the air base infrastructure. Two aircraft hangars served as our cycle shed, three blast pens bordered our playground, and the pathways between classrooms were disused taxiways. During lunch breaks, we played elaborate games of soldiers raiding an air base, inspired by stories of the approximately one hundred Pakistani commandos airdropped near Adampur during the 1965 Indo-Pak War. The Army and local civilians had apprehended those commandos before they could damage the strategic facility, but we were the undefeatable raiders raiding Pakistani bases!

Assassination and Aftermath

Then came October 30, 1984—a date that would mark another collision between our personal lives and national history. We were enjoying the annual school function that day. My best friend—a guy I had befriended just three months earlier—and I had invented a coded script in English and were passing notes about the performances (especially those by girls) in our secret language, chuckling at the puzzled expressions of classmates who couldn't decipher our messages.

The festivities came to an abrupt halt when the principal announced "chhutti" (holiday) and that the school would remain closed for the next few days. Rumours immediately circulated that somebody had shot Prime Minister Indira Gandhi. We dismissed these as false alarms—how could anyone penetrate the security perimeter that constantly surrounded the Prime Minister? It seemed impossible.

Upon reaching home, however, we discovered the rumours were true. More shocking still was the identity of the assassins—her own Sikh bodyguards. We had heard about some Sikh soldiers in the Army revolting during Operation Bluestar five months earlier, but had difficulty reconciling such actions with our understanding of military discipline. Now, the depth of hurt within the Sikh community following the Golden Temple operation had manifested in violence at the highest level of government.

The reaction was swift and devastating. Father returned that evening from duty with instructions for us to remain vigilant, as anti-Sikh riots had erupted in Delhi and across North India. We heard Sikhs in our vicinity celebrating Indira Gandhi's assassination with drums and bhangra—expressions of joy that seemed alien and disturbing to us, having been raised to respect authority figures regardless of political differences.

Fortunately, our family remained untouched by the violence that consumed other areas. The Sikh families in our village refrained from targeting military personnel and their families out of respect for "faujis" (soldiers), as almost every Sikh household had a family member serving in the armed forces, primarily the Army. This shared military identity provided a thin layer of protection amid sectarian hatred that was consuming communities elsewhere.

On that sombre autumn evening in 1984, our family gathered around our small black-and-white television, joining millions across India to witness Indira Gandhi's final journey. Though we sat hundreds of miles away in our modest Air Force quarters, something extraordinary happened as Rajiv Gandhi lit his mother's funeral pyre. The moment the flames leapt upward, consuming the sandalwood-draped body of our fallen Prime Minister, a peculiar scent of sandalwood wafted through our living room. Father looked at Mother, their eyes wide with disbelief—how could we possibly smell the funeral pyre from such a distance? Yet there it was, unmistakable and profound, as though the nation's collective grief had transcended physical boundaries to reach us. The next day, we watched as a pair of MiG-23s from our Adampur base escorted the An-12 heavy military transport aircraft carrying her ashes over the Himalayan peaks. At that moment, I understood something fundamental about belonging to a nation—how shared rituals of mourning could unite people who had never met, creating invisible bonds stronger than distance or difference. That strange olfactory connection to a leader's cremation remains one of the most inexplicable yet powerful memories of my childhood in military India, where the personal and the national often intertwined in ways both mysterious and profound.

Our stay at Adampur proved even briefer than our time in Amritsar—just four months. Father's unit relocated from Adampur to Ambala. We travelled in civilian trucks loaded with the unit's families' belongings, with men and older boys (including me) perched atop the luggage while women and younger children travelled in two Air Force buses.

I remember stopping for lunch at a roadside "dhaba," sitting on charpoys (traditional rope beds) while savouring tadka dal and tandoori roti. As we continued our journey towards Ambala, I sensed another transition approaching—not just of location but of identity. The time had come to transform from a child into a teenage rebel, leaving behind the wide-eyed innocence that had somehow survived even amid conflict zones and military operations.

Reflections on Coming of Age in Conflict

Looking back on this period from 1983 to early 1985, I recognise it as the true end of my childhood. While most adolescents experience a gradual transition from the sheltered perspectives of childhood to the more complex understandings of adulthood, mine came with the thunderclap of Operation Bluestar and its aftermath. The political became personal in ways that children in peaceful regions never experience.

The juxtaposition of ordinary childhood pleasures against extraordinary circumstances created cognitive dissonances that shaped my developing worldview. One day, I was flying in a training aircraft, experiencing the pure joy of seeing the world from above; days later, I was watching soldiers crawl across melting asphalt while bullets flew overhead. I invented secret codes with friends during a school function, only to have the event interrupted by news of a Prime Minister's assassination.

These experiences forced early reckonings with concepts most children encounter only abstractly, if at all: sectarian violence, terrorism, military necessity, collateral damage, and political assassination. I learned that religious identity could transform overnight from a matter of personal faith to a potential death sentence. I discovered that military precision—so impressive during air shows and parades—had a darker purpose in urban combat operations. I witnessed how quickly the social fabric could unravel when trust between communities collapsed.

Yet amid these harsh realities, the resilience of childhood asserted itself. We still played games, read comics, formed friendships, and found wonder in small discoveries like frozen dew on grass. The military structure that exposed us to danger also provided frameworks for processing it—routines resumed, schools reopened, transfers continued. Life moved forward with the inexorable momentum of service postings and academic calendars.

Perhaps most significantly, this period taught me that history isn't something that happens elsewhere to other people. History occurs where you stand, affecting your daily routines, school schedules, and family movements. The events described in textbooks and newspapers are experienced as lived reality by ordinary people—including children—who must navigate their personal development against backdrops of political upheaval and social transformation.

As our truck rumbled toward Ambala that day in the winter cold of early 1985, I wasn't just travelling to a new posting; I was moving toward a new understanding of myself in relation to a complex and often violent world. The child who had once played at being a paratrooper dropped behind enemy lines had, in some sense, actually experienced a premature deployment into adult realities. The teenage rebellion awaiting me in Ambala would be informed by these experiences—less innocent than it might have been, perhaps, but also more aware of the genuine costs of conflict and the actual value of peace.

Chapter 3

Brass Tacks and Broken Hearts: A Teenager in Uniform

Modest Beginnings in Ambala

The winter of 1985 brought us to Ambala, a city whose military significance dated back to the British colonial era. By the mid-1980s, Ambala was an important military base that included the headquarters of the "Kharga" Corps—the premier strike corps of the Indian Army comprising an armoured division, two infantry divisions, an independent mechanised brigade with complements of artillery, engineers, signals, air-defence artillery, and other support elements. The airbase had one MiG-21 air defence squadron—the "Hawks" (my father's maintenance sub-unit shared maintenance infrastructure with that squadron) —and two Jaguar deep-penetration strike fighter squadrons—the "Tuskers" and the "Bulls". After the tumultuous experiences in Punjab, this posting initially promised a return to normalcy—though I would soon discover that "normal" in military life always carried its own unique complexities. Our first accommodation was modest, civilian-rented accommodation: a simple one-room set with a small mezzanine that somehow managed to contain our family's life.

Despite the confined space—or perhaps because of it—we found creative ways to enjoy ourselves. Cricket matches with a plastic ball and a washerman's wooden bat became a regular pastime, the limited dimensions of our quarters adding an extra challenge that required precision and control rather than power. We developed an intricate system of scoring that accounted for our spatial constraints: hitting the ceiling was an automatic out, striking the back wall counted as a single, reaching the side walls earned two runs, and connecting with the front wall (without hitting the ceiling first) scored four. A direct hit to the small window above the front door—a feat requiring exceptional accuracy—earned six runs and bragging rights for days.

"Watch this," I would announce to my brother before attempting a particularly ambitious shot. "Kapil Dev special coming up!" More often than not, these declarations of intent would result in an embarrassing miss or an easy catch, but occasionally I would connect perfectly, sending the plastic ball precisely where I had aimed and prompting exaggerated celebrations modelled after those we had seen during televised matches.

The mezzanine room became a sanctuary of sorts, where I would follow my father's example and practise meditation, seeking the inner stillness that seemed so elusive amid the constant noise of military life. This small space, accessible by a narrow staircase going to the roof, offered a rare opportunity for privacy in our crowded quarters. I would sit cross-legged on a service darri (provided by the Air Force), attempting to clear my mind while the sounds of family life continued below—my mother preparing meals, my brother studying or playing, my father listening to All India Radio news bulletins. Though my teenage attempts at meditation rarely achieved profound spiritual insights, the practice introduced me to the value of intentional solitude and internal reflection—skills that would prove valuable throughout life's challenges.

The journey to school each morning was an adventure in itself. We travelled in an Air Force Shaktiman truck that had been modified with wooden benches to accommodate children. This makeshift school bus collected students bound for various institutions—Kendriya Vidyalaya (KV) No. 1, 2, and 3 (I was in KV No. 2), as well as a local convent school. The vehicle's suspension was minimal, transforming every pothole and speed bump into a potential launchpad that could send unwary passengers airborne. We quickly learned to grip the wooden benches firmly when approaching rough patches, our bodies developing an intuitive rhythm that anticipated and compensated for the truck's violent movements.

The social hierarchy among schoolchildren manifested clearly during these rides. The convent students carried themselves with an air of superiority, proud of their "English medium" education, while we KV students embraced our more desi identity. They would converse in carefully enunciated English, discussing Western music and fashion, while we deliberately spoke in Hindi, peppered with colourful slang that showcased our comfort with local culture.

"Look at them," my friend would mutter in Hindi as a group of convent girls boarded the truck in their crisp uniforms. "They think they're Angrezon ki Aulaad (children of the British)."

We would tease them in vernacular slang that often left them flustered, their polished English retorts proving ineffective against our earthy humour. These daily exchanges were more than childish banter—they represented competing visions of India itself: the Anglicised elite versus those more rooted in indigenous traditions. Never in my wildest dreams could I imagine that in another fifteen years I would end up having a convent-educated girl as my life partner!

Within a few months of our arrival, we moved to temporary Air Force quarters at ML Lines—a fascinating historical curiosity. These accommodations were originally constructed as horse stables in 1853 during the British colonial period and later converted into modest living quarters for Air Force families. The structure retained many vestiges of its original purpose, with a roof covered in long grass and toilets located outside the main living space, alongside the entrance. The walls were thick stone, providing excellent insulation against both summer heat and winter cold—a practical feature that compensated somewhat for the unusual layout.

The quarters consisted of two large rooms that had once housed horses, now partitioned with furniture to create separate areas for sleeping, dining, and relaxation. The ceiling was high and arched, with exposed wooden beams that had supported hay storage in colonial times. During monsoon season, small leaks would develop in the grass roof, requiring strategically placed buckets and pans to catch the dripping water. Rather than viewing these as inconveniences, my brother and I treated them as part of the adventure of living in a historical structure—each new leak prompting excited exploration to find suitable containers before water could damage our belongings.

While the quarters themselves were basic, their location offered an unexpected privilege that thrilled my aviation-obsessed heart. The most exciting feature of our new home was its alignment with the runway. We quickly discovered that by climbing onto the roof of the toilet block—using the main door and the pipes jutting from the water tanks as improvised handholds—we could access a spectacular vantage point overlooking the entire length of the runway stretching westward. This unofficial observation deck became our private airshow venue, offering views that aviation enthusiasts would have paid handsomely to enjoy.

"Come quickly!" I would call my brother whenever I heard the distinctive sound of aircraft engines spooling up for takeoff. "Jaguars are getting ready to take off!"

We would scramble up our improvised climbing route, positioning ourselves on the flat roof of the toilet block with unobstructed views of the runway. From this perch, we could observe every detail of flight operations: ground crew conducting final checks, pilots receiving clearance, aircraft taxiing into position, and finally the breathtaking moment of afterburners engaged, rapid acceleration, and liftoff. Each aircraft type had its distinctive characteristics—the nimble MiG-21s with their needle-like fuselages and delta wings, the sturdy Jaguars with their twin engines and low-wing configuration, and the occasional transport planes with their lumbering grace.

The Jaguars taking off in pairs at dusk for night-flying sorties provided a visual spectacle that no movie could match. The runway lights illuminating the darkness, the twin exhausts of each aircraft shooting flames with afterburners engaged, the thunderous roar as they accelerated down the runway directly into the setting sun before suddenly leaping skyward and disappearing into crimson clouds—this was cinema of the highest order, and we had front-row seats every evening. The vibration would travel through the ground and into our bodies, creating a physical connection to the machines that transcended mere observation. In those moments, I felt completely alive, every sense engaged as I witnessed these magnificent machines transition from earth to sky.

All aircraft landings in the afternoons would pass directly overhead, sometimes as low as 200 feet AGL (altitude from ground level) before touching down on the runway ahead. The fighters would fly so low that we could often glimpse the helmeted and masked faces of the pilots—a surreal connection between earth and sky. These brief moments of eye contact, though likely imagined on my part, created a sense of personal connection to the aviators who embodied my highest aspirations. Each landing approach became a lesson in aerodynamics as we observed how pilots adjusted to crosswinds, maintained proper glide paths, and executed the precise timing required to transition from flight to ground contact.

Different aircraft created different experiences. The MiG-21s were relatively manageable in terms of noise and disruption, but the twin-engine Jaguars would generate enough turbulence to rotate our television antenna, necessitating frequent climbs to the roof to realign it and restore our precious Doordarshan (DD) transmission. These adjustments became so routine that I developed an intuitive understanding of antenna positioning, able to achieve optimal reception through minor adjustments that considered both signal direction and the prevailing patterns of aircraft interference.

The most dramatic encounter came when the newly arrived Gajraj strategic heavy-lift transporters (the Soviet-built IL-76s) based at Chandigarh, less than ten minutes' flying time away, occasionally used our runway. I'll never forget the first time one of these massive aircraft approached Ambala, flying low over our quarters on its final approach. The sheer scale of the beast passing overhead created a sensation of primal fear—as though some ancient flying predator had returned to claim its territory. The shadow it cast momentarily darkened our entire living area, and the noise was so overwhelming that conversation became impossible until it had passed. The ground trembled beneath our feet, dishes rattled in the cupboards, and the television antenna needed to be completely repositioned after the turbulence subsided.

"That," my father explained with professional admiration, "is what real air power looks like." He described how these enormous aircraft could transport tanks, artillery pieces, and hundreds of troops across vast distances, projecting military capability far beyond national borders. This perspective helped me understand that the fighter jets I admired for their speed and agility represented only one aspect of air power—the strategic lift capability embodied by the IL-76 was equally crucial for national defence, though less glamorous in the eyes of aviation-obsessed teenagers.

Finding Purpose in Air NCC

The defining experience of my time at Ambala was joining the Air Wing of the National Cadet Corps (NCC) in class 8. This two-year junior division training programme provided structure, purpose, and a sense of belonging that resonated deeply with my military upbringing. The NCC combined elements of military discipline with character development, physical training, and basic aviation knowledge—a perfect blend for a teenager already immersed in Air Force culture but seeking his own identity within it.

My first visit to the firing range located within the air base for .22 rifle shooting practice remains etched in my memory. We assembled early in the morning, receiving detailed safety briefings before being issued rifles and ammunition under strict supervision. The range itself was positioned inside the airfield perimeter, allowing clear views of flight operations while we awaited our turns at the firing line. While the official purpose was marksmanship training, we cadets were equally interested in watching the MiGs and Jaguars taking off and landing nearby—especially the landings, when the brake parachutes would blossom behind the aircraft as they touched down, creating billowing white clouds that gradually collapsed as the aircraft decelerated.

'Eyes on your targets, cadets!' the instructor would bark whenever our attention drifted skyward. 'Those planes will still be flying when you've finished your rounds. Focus!'

When my turn came for the 'fire at will' exercise with ten rounds, I braced myself for recoil that never materialised—the .22 rifle being considerably gentler than I had anticipated. Nevertheless, the instructor barked orders with military precision: dig both heels into the ground while in the prone position; align the foresight, back aperture sight, rifle butt, right shoulder, right hip, and the entire length of the right leg with heels firmly planted; position the target at 25 yards; spread the left leg wide with heels dug in for stability. This firing position became so deeply ingrained in my muscle memory that even four decades later, I can instantly assume the stance and maintain rock-solid stability (though my expanded midsection now somewhat compromises the perfect alignment).

'Breathe normally,' the instructor advised as I prepared to fire my first round. 'Then exhale halfway, hold your breath, and squeeze—don't pull—the trigger.' The distinction between squeezing and pulling seemed academic until I tried both approaches and discovered the significant difference in accuracy. A gentle, progressive squeeze allowed the discharge to come as a surprise, preventing the anticipatory flinch that ruined aim when consciously pulling the trigger.

My first five shots formed a loose grouping near the centre of the target—respectable but not exceptional. The instructor made minor adjustments to my position, suggesting I relax my left shoulder slightly and maintain more consistent pressure with my cheek against the stock. The next five rounds clustered noticeably tighter, earning a nod of approval that felt more rewarding than effusive praise might have been. This pattern—incremental improvement through precise technical adjustments rather than dramatic breakthroughs—characterised much of my NCC training and shaped my approach to skill development throughout life.

Beyond marksmanship, the NCC taught me practical skills that bridged military discipline with everyday life: pressing a starched cotton uniform to crisp perfection; properly affixing shoulder badges; using Brasso to shine cap badges and belt buckles to a mirror finish; applying a small amount of saliva with shoe polish to achieve a gleaming shine on boots. These tasks, seemingly mundane, instilled attention to detail and pride in presentation that transferred to other aspects of life. The process of preparing my uniform became a meditative ritual — measuring precise alignment of the cap, ensuring perfect alignment of insignia, creating knife-edge creases in knee-length and starched cotton shorts — that connected me to generations of service members who had performed these same actions.

Perhaps most enduring was the distinctive gait and automatic synchronisation of pace when walking with others — a habit that persisted well into my early professional career, occasionally prompting colleagues to remind me, 'We're not on a military parade!' This unconscious tendency to match steps with companions, maintaining precise spacing and rhythm, became so natural that civilian environments sometimes felt chaotically uncoordinated by comparison. Years later, I would find myself instinctively adjusting my pace to match others during business meetings or social gatherings, a vestigial behaviour from those formative NCC days.

The pinnacle of my NCC experience came in October 1986 when I attended a ten-day Annual Training Camp (ATC) at Sainik School, Kunjpura, Karnal, about two hours by road from Ambala. At fourteen years old, this marked my first extended stay away from home—a significant milestone in my journey towards independence. The selection process had been competitive, with only the most dedicated and disciplined cadets chosen to represent our school. Being among the select few (only ten cadets chosen from sixty in our school) conferred special privileges, including two sets of uniform, extra socks, and a pair of parade boots with horseshoes clipped to the heels and toes.

These specialised boots produced a satisfying metallic sound while walking—a sound we cadets adored for the attention it commanded, particularly from the girls in our school. The distinctive 'click-clack' announced our presence before we were visible, creating an aura of importance that appealed to teenage vanity. It felt like wearing regalia, announcing our presence with every step. We would deliberately take longer routes through school corridors to maximise exposure, walking with exaggerated precision to amplify the metallic percussion of our footfalls.

'Here come the NCC boys,' classmates would whisper as we approached, the sound of our boots heralding our arrival like a military drumbeat. The mixture of admiration, curiosity, and occasional eye-rolling that greeted these entrances only enhanced our sense of special status—we were set apart, marked by both uniform and sound as belonging to something exclusive and prestigious.

However, this distinction came with an unexpected long-term consequence. The horseshoe nails protruding into the shoes caused me to develop painful corns on my toes and heels—an affliction that continues to trouble me when walking barefoot or in flat slippers, even forty years later. This physical reminder of my NCC days has accompanied me through life, a small but persistent pain that connects my adult self to that proud teenage cadet. The discomfort serves as a tangible link to that formative period, a bodily memory more durable than photographs or certificates.

The camp routine was rigorous but rewarding: reveille at 0500 hours, followed by physical training in the crisp morning air; breakfast in the mess hall with strict protocols for seating, serving, and clearing; classes on aviation principles, map reading, and military history; drill practice under the unforgiving midday sun; sports and team competitions in the afternoon; evening parade and flag-lowering ceremony as the day cooled; cultural activities and inter-squadron competitions after dinner; lights out at 2200 hours with absolute silence enforced thereafter.

Mess drills taught discipline in communal dining—entering in formation, standing behind chairs until the command to be seated, maintaining proper posture and conversation volume, using utensils correctly, and leaving only when dismissed by the duty officer. These formalities, which might seem excessive in civilian contexts, instilled an appreciation for order and collective harmony that extended beyond mealtimes. We learned that individual comfort sometimes needed to be subordinated to group efficiency, a lesson with applications far beyond military settings.

Kit layouts in the morning and before bedtime instilled attention to detail and organisation. Each item of clothing and equipment had its designated position on the bed, arranged according to precise specifications that could be inspected at a glance. Folding techniques ensured uniform dimensions for each garment, creating a visual harmony across the dormitory when all beds displayed their occupants' belongings. The practical value of this systematic approach became apparent whenever we needed to locate specific items quickly or pack efficiently for movement—skills that would prove useful throughout life's transitions.

Washing utensils after dinner reinforced the dignity of labour regardless of social background. Cadets from affluent families who had never performed household chores worked alongside those accustomed to such tasks, all subject to the same standards of cleanliness and efficiency. The shared experience levelled artificial distinctions, creating bonds based on present performance rather than previous privilege. I noticed how quickly complaints about "servant's work" disappeared when everyone—regardless of family background—participated equally in these essential duties.

Evening singing sessions built camaraderie and cultural connection through shared music. We learned patriotic songs, folk melodies from various regions of India, and military marching tunes that synchronised our voices just as drill had synchronised our movements. The progression from awkward, disjointed attempts to harmonious collective performance mirrored our development as a cohesive unit—individual voices finding their place within the greater whole without losing their distinctive qualities. These sessions often concluded with impromptu talent showcases where cadets would perform regional songs or dances, expanding our cultural awareness beyond our home states.

I volunteered for quarter guard duty during the camp, which meant staying in the quarter guard tent rather than the dormitories where most cadets slept—an assignment that felt adventurous and important, entrusted with maintaining security and protocol. The quarter guard served ceremonial functions—raising and lowering flags, receiving visiting officers with appropriate honours—while also maintaining practical security through regular patrols and checkpoint operations. This dual responsibility taught me that symbolism and substance were not opposing concepts but complementary aspects of effective systems.

The night shifts were particularly memorable, with three-hour watches that required maintaining alertness while most of the camp slept. During these quiet hours, I would contemplate the stars visible through the tent flap, listen to the distant sounds of nocturnal wildlife, and occasionally exchange whispered conversations with fellow guards about our homes, aspirations, and experiences. These midnight discussions, free from the structured activities that filled our days, created intimate connections that transcended regional and linguistic differences.

Our squadron won first prize in the drill competition—a testament to our precision and teamwork—and I personally secured first place in General Service Knowledge, demonstrating my absorption of military and Air Force information. These achievements reinforced my sense of belonging within the military ecosystem, validating both my heritage and personal aptitude. The certificates and medals we received, while modest in objective terms, represented significant milestones in our development as potential leaders and citizens.

One of the most challenging experiences during the camp was a route march to a flying club located five kilometres away. We departed early in the morning, marching in formation while singing cadence calls that maintained our pace and spirits. The outbound journey was manageable, with excitement about our destination providing motivation through occasional discomfort. The flying club rewarded us with views of Pushpak microlight trainers—beautiful, shining, yellow aircraft that immediately transported me back to my first flying experience with my brother at Amritsar.

We watched training flights with technical commentary from our instructors, who explained the principles of flight and basic manoeuvres being demonstrated. For most cadets, this was their first close encounter with actual aircraft, and the experience reinforced their interest in aviation. For me, having already experienced flight firsthand, the visit deepened my understanding of the technical aspects while reviving emotional memories of that magical day at Raja Sansi airport.

The return journey, however, tested our physical limits and moral character when we were ordered to run the entire five-kilometre distance back to camp. What began as an enthusiastic sprint quickly settled into a sustainable pace for most cadets, but the cumulative fatigue of the day's activities began to take its toll as we approached the halfway point. Breathing became laboured, legs grew heavy, and the formation began to stretch as faster runners pulled ahead while others struggled to maintain pace.

During this gruelling return, one of my fellow cadets developed severe cramps in his thighs. His face contorted with pain as he attempted to continue, his pace slowing dramatically despite obvious determination. Without hesitation, another cadet and I positioned ourselves on either side of him, supporting his weight as he hung from our shoulders. The three of us completed the distance in this awkward formation—running became limping, sweat poured freely, knees and calves screamed in protest, and the nails from our parade boots bit into our feet.

"Leave me," he gasped at one point. "You'll fail inspection if you're late."

"Not happening," I replied between laboured breaths. "We finish together or not at all."

We arrived at Sainik School Kunjpura well after the rest of our squadron had returned, but the delay carried no shame. Instead, we felt profound pride in having honoured the military ethos that "the Indian Army leaves no man behind." In that moment of shared struggle and solidarity, we felt we had truly earned the izzat (respect) embodied in the uniform we wore. Our squadron commander, rather than reprimanding us for tardiness, used our actions as an example during the evening briefing, emphasising that leadership meant prioritising the welfare of team members above individual achievement or comfort.

This experience taught me more about military values than any classroom lecture could have conveyed. The abstract principles of sacrifice, solidarity, and service became concrete through physical exertion and conscious choice. I understood that the true measure of training wasn't found in perfect performance under ideal conditions but in maintaining core values when circumstances became challenging. This lesson would resurface throughout my life, informing decisions in professional, personal, and civic contexts where principle and convenience came into conflict.

School Life and National Identity

The morning assembly at KV No.2, Ambala Cantt. was a ritual that transcended mere administrative function, becoming instead a daily affirmation of national identity and cultural heritage. We would march from our classrooms to the assembly ground in orderly files while the school band played drums, side drums, and flutes, creating a soundtrack that transformed ordinary students into participants in something greater than themselves. The precision of our movements, synchronised to the rhythmic percussion, created a visual and auditory harmony that prepared us mentally for the ceremonial aspects to follow.

The assembly began with a Rashtriya salute (national salute) accompanied by a resounding cry of "Jai Hind," followed by a brief musical interlude from the band. At the sound of a single drumbeat, we would lower our hands to the attention position with military precision. This was followed by "Teen Kaumi Naarey" (three national calls) as we shouted "Bharat Mata ki Jay" in unison. The collective voice of hundreds of students proclaiming these phrases created a powerful sense of shared identity and purpose that transcended individual differences of religion, language, or regional origin.

The morning prayer began and ended with hymns from the Rig Veda, connecting our modern educational experience to ancient traditions thousands of years old. These Sanskrit verses, though not fully understood by most students in their literal meaning, created a sense of continuity with India's intellectual and spiritual heritage. The prayer typically included universal themes of seeking knowledge, wisdom, and moral guidance rather than sectarian religious content, an approach that allowed students of all faiths to participate without compromise to their personal beliefs.

After these ceremonial elements came the practical components: a student reading the morning news, the thought for the day, announcements from the principal, and finally the national anthem, with the band again providing musical accompaniment to Jana Gana Mana. The entire assembly lasted approximately twenty minutes, but its impact extended throughout the day, establishing a framework of shared values and collective identity that informed our interactions and activities.

In today's political climate, such practices might be labelled as "ultra-nationalist" or "right-wing fanatic," but for us children—regardless of our religious and ethnic backgrounds—these rituals created a sense of connection to both the nation our fathers defended in uniform and the millennia-old continuity of Indian civilisation. This connection felt natural and uncontroversial, something we accepted without debate or question. The diversity within our student body—children from all regions of India, following various religious traditions—participated equally in these ceremonies, finding common ground in shared citizenship rather than division in particular identities.

The Annual Inspection at school elevated these everyday practices to spectacular proportions. This elaborate affair featured drill displays with marching contingents from classes 9, 10, 11, and 12, alongside platoons of Girl Guides, Boy Scouts, Girls Wing NCC (Army Wing), and Boys Wing NCC (Air Wing). Each group wore distinctive uniforms and performed specialised marching routines that showcased their training and discipline. The precision of these movements, practised for weeks in advance, created geometric patterns across the parade ground that could only be fully appreciated from the elevated platform where inspecting officers and school administrators sat.

Following the march past came mass physical training demonstrations, yoga displays, dumbbell exercises performed by junior classes, gymnastics (including the dramatic feat of jumping through a ring of fire), and group singing performances. These activities highlighted different aspects of student development—physical fitness, mental discipline, courage, coordination, and artistic expression—presenting education as a holistic process rather than merely academic instruction. Parents and community members would attend these events, creating a sense of public accountability and celebration that motivated students to perform at their best.

The Kendriya Vidyalaya song was a fixture at these events, along with patriotic standards like "Hind Desh Kay Niwasi" and "Saare Jahan Se Acchha." When singing the Kendriya Vidyalaya anthem, I would feel a surge of pride at the lyrics—"Bharat ka Swarnim Gaurav Kendriya Vidyalaya Layega, Takshashila Nalanda ka Itihaas Laut Kar Ayega" (Central School will bring back the pride of India's golden past, bringing back the history of Takshashila and Nalanda—ancient Indian universities that predated Oxford and Cambridge by millennia). This civilisational connection to millennia-old centres of knowledge still gives me goosebumps, reinforcing my understanding of India as fundamentally a knowledge-based civilisation whose contributions to human learning have been systematically undervalued in conventional historical narratives.

The song's references to these ancient universities weren't merely nostalgic invocations of past glory but aspirational statements about the potential for contemporary educational excellence rooted in indigenous traditions. As students of a system established after independence, we were positioned as inheritors of both ancient wisdom and modern scientific knowledge, a synthesis that rejected false dichotomies between tradition and progress. This perspective encouraged us to view education not as a colonial import but as the continuation of India's long intellectual history, adapted to contemporary needs but maintaining essential continuity with cultural roots.

Our education included practical lessons in the dignity of labour through seemingly mundane responsibilities. Each weekday, two students in each class (assigned according to a duty roster organised by roll number) would remain behind during morning assembly to clean the classroom—sweeping the floor, dusting furniture, and wiping window glass panes. This system ensured that all students, regardless of socioeconomic background, participated equally in maintaining their learning environment. The rotation of duties prevented any individual from feeling singled out for these tasks while ensuring that everyone experienced the satisfaction of contributing to collective well-being.

We regularly participated in "Shramdaan" (voluntary labour) to clear the school grounds of tall grass and weeds after monsoon rains. These sessions typically occurred on Saturday afternoons, with students bringing tools from home or using equipment provided by the school. Working in teams, we would transform overgrown areas into usable spaces for sports and outdoor activities. The physical exertion, shared purpose, and visible results created a sense of ownership and accomplishment that formal academic work sometimes lacked. These experiences taught practical problem-solving, teamwork, and the relationship between effort and outcome in ways that theoretical instruction could not match.

One particularly memorable instance of collective problem-solving occurred before an inter-school sports tournament when heavy rains had flooded our playing field. Rather than accepting postponement, we students devised an ingenious solution: digging a shallow trench in the field where water had collected, then forming a human chain from this trench to the school garden nearby. Bucket by bucket, we transferred water from the flooded area to the garden. Within half an hour, the ground was sufficiently drained; we then filled the trench and levelled it, feeling immense pride in our resourcefulness and teamwork.

The experience demonstrated several valuable lessons: identifying the core problem (excess water in a specific location rather than general dampness); developing a practical solution with available resources; organising collective effort efficiently; and persisting through physical discomfort to achieve a desired outcome. These principles would prove applicable in countless situations throughout life, from professional challenges to community initiatives. The satisfaction of watching our waterlogged field transform into a playable surface through our own efforts provided motivation more powerful than any external reward could have offered.

I'm often astonished by contemporary attitudes that consider such activities beneath students' dignity. When parents and children today express outrage at teachers asking students to participate in cleaning or maintenance activities, I wonder what kind of citizens such entitlement produces. The lessons we learned through physical labour—resourcefulness, cooperation, respect for all forms of work—proved as valuable as any academic subject in preparing us for life's challenges. The integration of mental and manual work created a balanced educational experience that recognised multiple forms of intelligence and contribution, rather than privileging abstract knowledge over practical capability.

This approach reflected Gandhi's concept of "Nai Taleem" (new education), which emphasised learning through productive work rather than separating intellectual development from physical labour. Though our school system wasn't explicitly Gandhian, elements of this philosophy informed practices that connected classroom learning to practical application and community service. The result was an education that prepared us not just for examinations but for citizenship—developing capabilities and attitudes necessary for contributing to collective welfare rather than merely pursuing individual advancement.

Intellectual Awakening and Political Consciousness

Although I demonstrated aptitude in Mathematics and Science, particularly Physics, my true intellectual passion lay in History. The systematic study of human experience across time and space offered perspectives that technical subjects, for all their precision, could not provide. When our curriculum in classes 9 and 10 introduced world history, I became fascinated by the ancient civilisations of Africa and America. The architectural achievements of Great Zimbabwe, the mathematical innovations of the Maya, the sophisticated urban planning of Mohenjo-daro — these examples contradicted simplistic narratives of progress that positioned Western Europe as the singular source of significant human advancement.

I felt a sense of moral outrage at how Western supremacist approaches had systematically erased or minimised these civilisations, creating an identity crisis for contemporary Africans and Native Americans who had been disconnected from their historical achievements and cultural legacies. The parallels with

India's colonial experience were obvious—the systematic devaluation of indigenous knowledge systems, the imposition of foreign standards of value, the creation of educational structures that privileged imported perspectives over local wisdom. This recognition fostered solidarity with other formerly colonised peoples and a critical perspective on historical narratives that served imperial interests.

The history of the Russian Revolution captured my imagination, particularly how the Soviet Union developed during the 1920s and 1930s while the rest of the world suffered through the Great Depression. The rapid industrialisation, universal literacy campaigns, and scientific advancements achieved under challenging circumstances suggested alternative development models to the capitalist paradigm that dominated global economics. I found equally compelling the story of how the United States leveraged its geographical advantages to generate unprecedented wealth during World War II, while other nations endured destruction. The contrast between these trajectories raised questions about structural advantages in the international system that persisted beyond formal colonial relationships.

I credit my history teacher, Bakshi sir, with introducing me to Marxist-Leninist philosophy — an interest my father encouraged, having himself participated in communist student movements during his youth in late-1950s Bengal. Bakshi Sir's approach to historical analysis emphasised material conditions and power structures rather than individual personalities or isolated events. He encouraged us to identify patterns across different historical periods and geographical regions, and to develop analytical frameworks that could be applied to contemporary situations. His teaching style combined rigorous factual information with interpretive questions that required us to evaluate evidence and construct arguments—skills that transcended the specific content of history courses.

My father's support for this intellectual exploration reflected his own complex relationship with leftist thought. Though he served in the military—an institution often associated with conservative values—he maintained progressive views on economic justice, social equality, and anti-imperialism. His experiences in late-1950s Bengal during periods of political turmoil had exposed him to various ideological perspectives, but he had actively participated in leftist students' movements. Hence, he encouraged me to engage critically with different systems of thought rather than uncritically accept any single framework. Our evening discussions often centred on historical events and their contemporary implications, with my father challenging my emerging interpretations while respecting my intellectual autonomy.

During this period, Soviet books were readily available in local bookstores, and I quickly amassed an extensive collection at home. These publications — ranging from simplified explanations of dialectical materialism to detailed analyses of economic systems — were heavily subsidised by the Soviet cultural programme, making them more affordable than Western publications. The books featured high-quality paper, excellent illustrations, and accessible translations, explicitly designed to appeal to young readers in developing nations. This material accessibility facilitated intellectual exploration that might otherwise have been prohibitively expensive for a middle-class military family.

Together with like-minded school friends, I began dreaming of revolution in India—overthrowing what we perceived as a British-designed, exploitative system and creating a more just society with a strong economy and defence capabilities that could resist Western hegemony. Our adolescent discussions combined genuine moral concern for social inequality with romantic notions of revolutionary heroism, often failing to fully appreciate the complex realities and potential costs of radical social transformation. We would meet during lunch breaks or after school, sketching ambitious plans for restructuring Indian society while lacking a practical understanding of governance, economics, or the diverse interests that would need to be accommodated in any viable political project.

My reading expanded to include revolutionary guerrilla warfare tactics from around the world and American military countermeasures, as I developed theories for neutralising such Western approaches. I studied accounts of the Vietnamese resistance against American forces, the Cuban Revolution, and various anti-colonial struggles in Africa, analysing the strategies that allowed numerically and qualitatively inferior forces to prevail against better-equipped opponents. This interest wasn't merely academic—I genuinely believed that such knowledge might prove necessary if India faced renewed imperial aggression or internal counter-revolutionary violence. The military environment in which I lived made such scenarios seem more plausible than they might have to teenagers in purely civilian contexts.

I also became interested in the geopolitics of oil and its influence on global power structures and economic interests. The relationship between petroleum resources and international conflicts fascinated me—how access to energy shaped military capabilities, economic development, and diplomatic leverage. In the late 1980s, I couldn't have known that we would soon witness bloody oil-driven power struggles in the Gulf and Middle East, but my teenage readings had prepared me to understand these conflicts when they erupted. This early interest in resource geopolitics provided analytical tools that would help me interpret subsequent international developments through a more sophisticated lens than mainstream media narratives typically offered.

Then came the seismic shifts of 1989–90, when my romantic revolutionary ideals collided with historical reality. Initially, terms like Perestroika and Glasnost were merely vocabulary to memorise for general knowledge examinations. But soon I was confronted with television and magazine images of Lenin's statues being toppled in Moscow and across Eastern Europe, country after country shedding communist governance, horrific accounts of mass genocides emerging from former communist regimes (under Pol Pot, Ceauşescu, and Stalin's political purges), and the Berlin Wall falling into rubble.

These developments forced me to question whether the ideal of a just and equal society was merely a utopian fantasy. The global collapse of communism troubled me deeply throughout my twenties and early thirties, until I gradually came to understand that each civilisation is hardwired with unique thought patterns and cultural preferences. Attempting to impose seemingly efficient systems from one cultural context onto another often leads to civilisational disaster — a lesson that tempered my youthful idealism with a more nuanced appreciation for organic social development.

Witnessing the Human Cost of Service

During this period, my father's health deteriorated, and he was diagnosed with ischemic heart disease (IHD). He spent many days in the large Military Hospital (MH) near our quarters. These hospital visits created an unexpected culinary opportunity that appealed to my teenage appetite: I would carry homemade food to him during evening visiting hours, then wait outside until darkness fell and the hospital served dinner. My father, having already eaten the food from home, would surreptitiously fill my tiffin container with the hospital's mutton curry before sneaking out to hand it over. My brother and I would savour this contraband feast at home during our own dinner, continuing my childhood appreciation for military hospital cuisine that had begun during my jaundice treatment at the naval hospital years earlier.

Beyond these small adventures, my visits to the Military Hospital revealed the human cost of maintaining national security. Ambala, as a major military base, received numerous casualties from the Siachen Glacier for treatment. Through these encounters, I learned about "Operation Meghdoot", which had commenced in the summer of 1985, pitting Indian Army soldiers against Pakistani forces in daily skirmishes at altitudes ranging from 18,000 to 22,000 feet in temperatures plunging below -50 degrees Celsius.

I would see young soldiers, barely out of their teens, with hands and legs amputated due to frostbite, facing uncertain futures yet maintaining remarkably high spirits. They shared stories of combat in those frozen heights, describing how they showed mercy to surrendered enemies while lamenting that Pakistani forces rarely reciprocated such humanity. These wounded warriors took pride in this distinction, viewing the Indian Army not merely as a fighting force but as a moral force whose conduct reflected national values even under extreme conditions.

The Ambala Military Hospital also treated casualties from "Operation Pawan" in Sri Lanka, where Indian Peace Keeping Force (IPKF) operations were ongoing. My father once encountered a retired Subedar visiting his injured son in an adjacent bed. The son, barely an adult, had taken a bullet to his neck during operations in Sri Lanka and was paralysed from the neck down. The retired soldier lamented a cruel irony: he had served through the conflicts of 1962, 1965, and 1971 without sustaining a single injury, while his seventeen-year-old son—just beginning his life and military career—had been permanently disabled during his first combat deployment. This juxtaposition of fates highlighted the arbitrary nature of war's costs, where experience offered no guarantee of safety and youth no protection from catastrophic injury.

Operation Brass Tacks: War Games and Real Tensions

In January–February 1987, unusual military activity suggested something beyond routine exercises. While the Indian military typically conducted large-scale manoeuvres during this period each year, the scale and intensity of preparations indicated higher stakes. We witnessed unprecedented troop movements and frequent landings of heavy transport aircraft at Ambala, which served as headquarters for the premier "Kharga" Strike Corps.

A detachment of Mirage fighters from Gwalior deployed temporarily to Ambala, and I observed their impressive low-level, low-speed handling capabilities and extremely tight turning radius during practice dogfights with the base's MiG aircraft. Passive Air Defence (PAD) drills became frequent, with blackouts followed by low-level, high-speed mock bombing runs by Jaguar aircraft that physically shook our quarters despite our foreknowledge of their coming. MiGs would scramble to engage the Jaguars in simulated aerial combat, creating a constant soundtrack of jet engines and air raid sirens signalling "attack" and "all clear" conditions.

One evening, my father returned from duty with instructions for us to keep essential documents readily accessible for potential rapid evacuation. He helped us identify depressions in the ground near our quarters that could serve as improvised trenches during an air raid, knowledge he had acquired firsthand while under aerial attack at Halwara. Soon afterwards, television news confirmed what military families had already surmised: Indian and Pakistani forces were deployed in an eyeball-to-eyeball confrontation along the entire western border.

This was "Operation Brass Tacks", a massive military exercise that escalated into a near-war situation. Tensions eventually subsided in February following "cricket diplomacy" between Prime Minister Rajiv Gandhi and Pakistani President General Zia-ul-Haq. Years later, I learned that Exercise Brass Tacks had been conceived by then Chief of Army Staff General

Krishnaswamy Sundarji as a strategic feint, threatening to bisect Pakistan through Sindh with India's armoured strike corps while preparing for the actual objective: bold moves into Gilgit, just south of the Actual Ground Position Line in Siachen. The plan aimed to reclaim the northern portion of Pakistan-occupied Kashmir, though this operation never materialised. (Perhaps, I sometimes think, I might yet witness such a development in my lifetime.)

Terrorism and Counter-Terrorism

Although Khalistani terrorism in neighbouring Punjab had diminished in intensity, it remained an ongoing threat. Security forces were gradually gaining the upper hand, particularly after "Operation Night Dominance", launched by Punjab Director General of Police K. P. S. Gill. "Operation Black Thunder" had concluded successfully, demonstrating how lessons from Operation Bluestar had been incorporated into counter-terrorism doctrine. Unlike the earlier operation, "Black Thunder" was conducted with surgical precision by the newly established National Security Guard (NSG), resulting in no casualties among security forces, all terrorists apprehended alive, and minimal collateral damage.

Perhaps motivated by desperation as their movement lost momentum, Khalistani militants apparently planned a spectacular attack to regain media attention. One evening in mid-1987, we suddenly observed infantry troops deploying along the entire perimeter of the airbase. Our quarters at Pinto Lines bordered this perimeter fence, putting us close to whatever operation was unfolding. Military authorities issued strict instructions to the families to remain indoors, an order that triggered traumatic memories of my experiences during Operation Bluestar in Amritsar.

The situation intensified when Army Aviation Chetak helicopters began conducting low-altitude reconnaissance flights over the base, making repeated passes that suggested an active search operation. By nightfall, conditions had normalised without any public explanation. We later learned that two Khalistani terrorists had infiltrated the airbase, intending to damage aircraft and personnel, hoping to create an international media spectacle. Security forces had engaged and neutralised them before they could fire a single round.

This efficient response impressed me deeply, the "brutal efficiency of the Indian war machine", as I thought of it then, a trait that I still identify with, given my birth at the Air Force Hospital, Chakeri, Kanpur, in 1972. This organic connection to the Indian military, particularly the Air Force, has remained a core element of my identity throughout life. (Even now, I sometimes hope that when my time comes, I draw my final breath in a military or Air Force hospital, completing the circle that began with my birth in such a facility.)

Movies and Military Heroes

The Hollywood film "Top Gun" was released internationally in 1986 but reached Ambala theatres in 1987. As a fourteen-year-old aviation enthusiast, I was thrilled to watch it with friends at Kharga cinema hall (named for the Corps headquarters in Ambala). The venue offered special attractions beyond the film itself: balcony seating provided premium viewing, while the Army canteen offered snacks and fast food at remarkably affordable prices. An additional visual attraction for us teenage boys came in the form of officers' daughters dressed in fashionable spaghetti-strap tops and miniskirts, a stark contrast to the more conservative attire typical among families of non-commissioned personnel like ourselves.

Although "Top Gun" depicted naval aviation, my friends and I mentally transposed the scenarios to our familiar context, imagining ourselves piloting IAF MiGs in dogfights against Pakistani F-16s. (This adolescent fantasy would find remarkable validation thirty-two years later when Wing Commander Abhinandan Varthaman engaged and shot down a two-seater F-16 across the Line of Control in February 2019, an achievement that sceptics may dismiss as propaganda, but which military professionals on both sides privately know.)

Ambala had its own "Maverick" figure who embodied the fighter pilot mystique: Flight Lieutenant Ravi Khanna of the Tuskers squadron, who flew the Jaguar deep-penetration strike aircraft. Tall, fair-complexioned, and moustachioed, he cut a more impressive figure than Tom Cruise, especially when wearing Ray-Ban sunglasses with his flying overall while riding his Royal Enfield Bullet motorcycle around the base. For two consecutive years, he won the Air Force's best air-to-ground gunnery shield, cementing his status as our local hero and role model.

In a curious intersection of our lives, he married the sister of one of our classmates, whose father served as Station Logistics Officer, during our final year of school. Our entire class XII-A skipped school to attend her mehndi ceremony, an act of collective truancy that earned us mass punishment the next morning during assembly. But the connection to our aviator hero made the disciplinary consequences worthwhile.

Fate seems to maintain special vigilance over such exceptional individuals. Many years later, I learned that Wing Commander Ravi Khanna, by then commanding the Dragons squadron of maritime strike Jaguars, had died in a crash during a range-firing sortie at Pokhran in 2004. A technical malfunction caused bombs to detonate immediately upon release during a low-altitude bombing run. Without sufficient altitude or time to eject, Wingo Khanna perished with his aircraft while performing the precision bombing at which he excelled. The handsome young officer we had idolised in our adolescence had been reduced to charred lumps of flesh, a stark reminder of the mortal risks accepted by military aviators as an occupational reality.

Cultural Celebrations and Community Life

Durga Puja celebrations at Ambala created memories that have remained vivid across decades. Preparations would begin months in advance, with children and teenagers (aged 10–15) starting drama rehearsals two months before the festival. By the time of our performance on Shashthi (the first day of Durga Puja), we had memorised every character's dialogue. Sometimes my mother would participate in open-air theatrical productions (Jatra) with a similar rehearsal schedule.

The young unmarried colleagues of my father (known as "living-in" personnel) would spend evenings collecting donations and advertisements for the souvenir program, returning after the airmen's mess had closed for the night. My mother would cook dinner for them throughout the 2–3 months preceding the festival, extending our family's hospitality to these temporary bachelors.

Pandal construction would commence a few days before Puja, with volunteers working late shifts after completing their regular duties at the base. Again, my mother would prepare dinner for these men, creating an extended family atmosphere through shared meals.

The four days of Puja each year created a heady mixture of spiritual observance and social enjoyment: morning Pushpanjali (flower offerings), feasting on bhog-khichudi for lunch and dinner, lazy afternoons at the pandal listening to popular Bengali film songs while discussing which girls looked most attractive in their festival attire. During this period, my teenage friends and I were collectively infatuated with tennis star Steffi Graf, though my personal interest was heightened because my neighbourhood crush resembled her (minus the blonde hair).

Evenings featured cultural programs with plays performed by Air Force families, musical performances, and finally the grand procession carrying the idol throughout Ambala Cantonment before reaching the lake at Ambala City for immersion. We would return to the now-empty puja pandal for a concluding feast of mutton kasha and pulao. These celebrations coincided with autumn school breaks, allowing for unrestricted enjoyment without academic obligations.

The SNCO (Senior Non-Commissioned Officers) mess "kick-off parties" at Ambala provided another form of regular entertainment. Monthly transitions in mess administration were marked by social gatherings where the outgoing mess manager hosted families of all SNCOs. These events typically began with several rounds of Tambola (similar to Bingo), which my family rarely won despite regular participation. The number calling followed distinctive military patterns with humorous associations: "Bangladesh, Mujibur Rehman, Seven One, Seventy-One," "Cheeni Hamla (Chinese Attack), Six Two, Sixty-Two," "Yahya Khan, Six Five, Sixty-Five," "Ladki Cycle Pe (Girl on Bicycle), One Five, Fifteen," and so forth.

After Tambola, came film screenings on VCR (Video Cassette Recorder), while our dads enjoyed rum punch in the adjacent hall. The evening concluded with a buffet dinner served on immaculate Air Force mess crockery. My most vivid culinary memories include the aromatic pulao, fiery red chicken curry, and dessert of small gulab jamuns floating in custard—a combination that still triggers salivation decades later.

Adolescent Romance: Love Thy Neighbour

No teenage memoir would be complete without a love story, though mine qualifies more accurately as an unrequited crush. In December 1987, while preparing for board examinations scheduled for March 1988, a new family moved into neighbouring quarters. This Punjabi household had recently returned from London, where the father had been posted at the Office of the Indian Air Attaché. Among their children were two brothers and two sisters, with the eldest daughter approximately my age. She enrolled at Air Force School one class behind me, as the tenth-grade board examination curriculum covered material from both ninth and tenth grades, requiring her to complete the earlier coursework before attempting the board exams.

One glimpse was sufficient to trigger complete infatuation. She dressed more boldly than other girls in our Air Force neighbourhood and bore a striking resemblance to Steffi Graf, though with dark hair instead of blonde. During the year our families lived in proximity (before my father's term for service quarters expired), I existed in an alternate reality coloured by romantic preoccupation. I began to appreciate poetry and romantic songs with newfound depth. When the film Qayamat Se Qayamat Tak was released, I mentally cast her as Juhi Chawla's character and would play soundtrack cassettes whenever she took evening walks near our quarters.

My pursuit of physical fitness intensified, and I engineered opportunities to play cricket and badminton with her brothers, allowing brief, shy glances in her direction. After dinner, I would stroll in front of our quarters, hoping for a chance encounter, particularly during rainy evenings when I could justify wandering with an umbrella. Over the years, her facial features and voice have faded from memory, but certain sensory associations remain vivid: the fragrance of her talcum powder, the distinctive smell of eucalyptus trees lining the roads, and the peculiar aroma of congress grass (an invasive weed inadvertently imported with American food aid during the 1960s Congress government) that grew abundantly around our quarters.

Even now, this combination of scents can trigger that adolescent sensation of nervous anticipation—hoping for a glimpse of my crush while pretending nonchalance. The song "So Gaya Yeh Jahan..." from the 1988 film Tezaab became permanently associated with those post-dinner walks, creating a soundtrack to unrequited longing that has outlasted the specific details of its object.

Educational Transitions and Career Aspirations

By the time I reached twelfth grade, my classmates and I confronted the uncertainty awaiting us beyond school life. A common aspiration among male students from military families involved applying to the National Defence Academy (NDA) through examinations conducted by the Union Public Service Commission. Our entire class of thirty-five boys (minus the eight girls) appeared at the same examination centre in Chandigarh, creating a somewhat comical spectacle as we arrived with military-style crew cuts, polished boots, and the distinctive gait of young men who imagined themselves already reporting to NDA squadrons rather than an examination hall.

Despite our enthusiasm, none of us succeeded in that particular examination cycle. However, our shared military ambitions eventually bore fruit for several classmates: one gained admission to NDA the following year, opting for the Navy and becoming a naval aviator flying helicopters from both shore installations and warships; another joined the Navy as a logistics officer; and a third entered the Coast Guard, eventually commanding a ship and a Coast Guard base before receiving a posting to Coast Guard headquarters in Delhi, earning a Tat Rakshak Medal in January 2025 for distinguished service.

My own academic journey encountered an unexpected obstacle when I contracted a severe case of measles shortly before board examinations in March 1990. The illness was so debilitating that I couldn't open my eyes for two weeks. Despite this setback, I managed to appear for the examinations, though I failed Chemistry while passing three elective subjects (Mathematics, Physics, and Biology) along with English language. My overall score of just 50% was sufficient for admission to SD College Ambala Cantt. in Arts, where I selected Economics, Political Science, and English Literature as my subjects—a significant deviation from the science track I had previously followed.

After completing examinations, I joined two classmates for a "picnic" near the Tangri River (more accurately described as a modest stream). We cooked chicken and rice over an open fire using wild twigs for fuel, enjoyed wading in waist-deep muddy waters, and danced to Bollywood songs—particularly "Papa Kehtey Hain Badaa Naam Karega…" from the movie *Qayamat Se Qayamat Tak.* This celebration marked our transition from school life to divergent paths, though we couldn't have predicted the specific directions our lives would take.

The Haunted Church and Other Local Legends

An abandoned church near our school and quarters—constructed before the 1857 revolt and damaged by Pakistani bombing during the 1971 war when enemy pilots mistook it for the control tower due to its alignment with the runway—provided a setting for adolescent dares and ghost stories. By the late 1980s, the structure resembled something from a Western horror film: dilapidated walls, creaking wooden doors, broken window panes, and deteriorating stairs leading to the former bell tower.

Although authorities had prohibited entry to the dangerous structure and explicitly forbidden attempts to climb the unstable staircase, these restrictions merely enhanced its appeal to rebellious teenagers. We made frequent visits, deliberately timing our explorations during the gathering darkness at dusk to maximise atmospheric tension. Reaching the top of the structure became a rite of passage—a thrilling challenge accompanied by the eerie sounds of wind passing through the ruins and the unsettling creaks of aged wood bearing our weight.

We would speculate about potential supernatural presences, interpreting every unexpected sound as possible communication from restless spirits. This abandoned church has since been incorporated into the expanded campus of Air Force School, with the historic structure preserved within modern educational facilities—a transformation that has eliminated the delicious sense of forbidden danger that once made it so appealing to adventure-seeking adolescents.

Reflections on Military Childhood and Adolescence

As I approached the conclusion of my time in Ambala and prepared for the transition to college life, I found myself reflecting on the unique aspects of growing up within the military community. The constant exposure to aircraft, weapons, and uniformed personnel had normalised elements that civilians might find extraordinary. The regular sight of wounded soldiers from Siachen and Sri Lanka had given me an unvarnished understanding of service and sacrifice that most teenagers never encounter. The political upheavals I had witnessed—"Operation Bluestar", Indira Gandhi's assassination and its aftermath, "Operation Brass Tacks"—had intertwined national history with my personal narrative in ways impossible to disentangle.

Military childhood had bestowed both gifts and burdens. The frequent relocations had taught adaptability but sometimes at the cost of lasting friendships. The structured environment had instilled discipline while occasionally constraining the natural rebelliousness of adolescence. The hierarchical society of the Air Force station had shown me both the value of order and the arbitrary nature of status determined by rank rather than character.

Perhaps most significantly, growing up under the flight path had shaped my perception of danger and possibility. Those Jaguars taking off at dusk, afterburners glowing against the setting sun, represented both the threat of conflict and the triumph of human ingenuity. The wounded soldiers in Military Hospital embodied both the harsh realities of geopolitics and the resilience of the human spirit.

As I prepared to enter civilian college life, I recognised that my military upbringing had given me a perspective both broader and more grounded than many of my future classmates would possess. I had witnessed firsthand the human cost of national security, understood the practical meaning of service before self, and developed an instinctive respect for competence and discipline that would inform my approach to adult challenges. The Air Force hadn't just been my father's profession—it had been my education in citizenship and character, conducted not through textbooks but through the lived experience of a community dedicated to something larger than individual ambition.

Chapter 4
Mandal, Movies, and Military Drills: My College Awakening

The Unexpected Pivot

My journey into college life began with an academic stumble that would unexpectedly alter my trajectory. The end of school life came on an ominous note—I failed Chemistry and barely passed Mathematics and Biology, scoring an overall 50% in my board exams. One mark less and it would have been a Third Division! For a time, I existed in limbo, confused about whether I had passed or needed to repeat Class 12. Eventually, I learned that having passed three elective subjects (Mathematics, Physics, and Biology) along with English, I was officially "passed." However, failing Chemistry closed the door to science streams in graduation, as both PCM and PCB required the "C" that I now lacked.

What initially felt like an academic catastrophe soon revealed itself as serendipity. Without Chemistry anchoring me to the sciences, I could finally pursue Economics and English Literature—subjects that had always fascinated me but which I had abandoned in favour of science due to peer pressure and that uniquely Indian concern, "log kya kahengey" (what will people say). Like many teenagers, I had chosen my academic path based on what my friends were doing rather than following my own interests.

With this unexpected freedom, I secured admission to S.D. College in Ambala Cantt for a Bachelor of Arts with Economics, Political Science, and English Literature, with Hindi as a compulsory subject. The college's curious official name—S.D. College (Lahore) Ambala Cantt—served as a constant reminder of the subcontinent's unforgettable wound of Partition. Originally established in Lahore, the institution had been forced to relocate to Ambala after Independence, its very name—Sanatan Dharma College—making it unwelcome in the newly formed Islamic Republic of Pakistan.

The campus itself was a stark departure from the ordered environment of KVs (Kendriya Vidyalayas (central schools)). Instead of neatly trimmed lawns and disciplined corridors, S.D. College offered sprawling grounds often waterlogged during monsoons, crowded classrooms with over 70 students per class, and a freedom that felt both exhilarating and disorienting after years within the structured military environment.

For the first time in my life, I was stepping into a predominantly civilian space. While Ambala remained a cantonment town with a significant military presence, the college represented a different world—one where military hierarchy held no sway, where students came from diverse backgrounds beyond service families, and where the rhythms of life weren't dictated by parade grounds and air-raid sirens. This transition marked the beginning of my gradual integration into civilian society, though my military upbringing would continue to influence how I navigated this new terrain.

Freedom and Friendship

In college, I developed a friendship with a Punjabi classmate who had also migrated from the Science stream to the Arts stream and shared most of my subjects, except for Mathematics, which he took instead of Political Science. Unlike me, he possessed an entrepreneurial spirit, supplementing his education with part-time direct sales of home fire extinguishers. His romantic life provided endless entertainment—he had fallen for a senior student who liked him but was involved with someone else. Predictably, his favourite song that year was "Tu Pyaar Hai Kisi Aur Ka, Tujhe Chahta Koi Aur Hai" from the film *Dil Hai Ki Manta Nahi*—a perfect soundtrack for his unrequited affections.

This friendship introduced me to one of college's most cherished traditions: bunking classes to watch movies. One morning, as I arrived at college, my friend proposed skipping lectures to catch a new film that was generating buzz for its music and fresh-faced leads. We assumed our absence would go unnoticed in our massive class of over 70 students. However, upon entering the cinema for the morning show (selected for its cheaper tickets), we discovered almost our entire class already seated. The only difference was that they had arrived in couples, while we were two single guys attending what turned out to be an intensely romantic film.

We slipped into our seats as the title song played "Saanso Ki Zaroorat Hai Jaise..." from a movie called *Aashiqui*, which would soon become a cultural phenomenon. Watching this romantic drama surrounded by classmates who had also chosen entertainment over education created a strange sense of communal truancy. The experience taught me that college offered not just academic learning but also lessons in independence, decision-making, and occasionally, the art of strategic absence.

Another memorable adventure occurred during the monsoon season when heavy rains had flooded the college grounds. Restless and unwilling to remain confined to classrooms, my friend and I noticed a small elevated patch—barely two feet square—rising like an island in the middle of the inundated playground. Armed with an umbrella and a stool, we waded through ankle-deep water to claim this miniature territory.

Only after establishing ourselves on our improvised island did we realise we had become an unintentional spectacle. Classes had paused as students and teachers gathered at windows and corridors to watch the two idiots perched with an umbrella in the middle of a flooded field during a downpour. Our aquatic expedition became the talk of the college for days afterwards—not exactly the academic reputation I had envisioned, but certainly memorable.

These experiences represented my first taste of genuine freedom—the ability to make impulsive decisions, good or bad, without the immediate oversight that had characterised life on Air Force stations. While military bases had offered security and structure, college provided the space to experiment with identity and independence, even if that meant occasionally making a public spectacle of myself.

Tanks and Artillery: A Different Military Perspective

After finishing school, we moved to decent civilian accommodation near my new college, close to a large field used by the Army for various drills. Although I had grown up in Air Force environments, Ambala Cantt's position as headquarters of the "Kharga" Strike Corps meant a heavy Army presence throughout the area. My daily ten-minute walk to college (reduced to five minutes on my new Hero Ranger bicycle) provided unprecedented close-up exposure to Army operations that had previously been distant and unfamiliar.

Most fascinating were the drills conducted with Vijayanta tanks—the Indian version of British Vickers Mark-1 Main Battle Tanks. I would watch, mesmerised, as these mechanical behemoths swivelled their main guns backward while drivers manoeuvred in circles, creating the impression of disoriented beetles spinning madly in reverse. The combination of raw mechanical power and precise control was hypnotic, so different from the sleek aircraft that had dominated my childhood visual landscape.

My friend from college would join me as we observed artillery soldiers performing their distinctive kadam-taal (mark time) drills with air defence guns and the infamous Bofors—weapons that had become household names due to corruption allegations against former Prime Minister Rajiv Gandhi. Political controversies aside, the Bofors impressed me as an engineering marvel—the heaviest artillery piece in the Indian Army's arsenal at the time, capable of limited independent movement and introducing me to the concept of "shoot-and-scoot" tactics essential for survival against enemy counter-battery fire.

These observations provided a different perspective on military operations than my Air Force upbringing had offered. Where Air Force activities often occurred at a distance—aircraft taking off into the sky, disappearing from view—Army exercises unfolded at ground level, with visible human operators and mechanical systems working in coordinated harmony. This expanded my understanding of defence forces beyond the familiar blue uniforms and aircraft of my childhood, helping me appreciate the multi-dimensional nature of military operations.

Years later, during the Kargil War of 1999, I would recall these observations when news reports highlighted the devastating effectiveness of Bofors artillery against Pakistani positions in the mountains. The weapons that had become political liabilities proved their military worth when it mattered most—a reminder that equipment should ultimately be judged by its performance in the field rather than controversies in parliamentary debates.

The Mandal Commission: Political Awakening

The most significant event during my college years was the anti-Mandal Commission students' movement that engulfed northern India in early autumn 1990. Until then, India had maintained a system of 25% reservation in educational institutions (except minority institutions) and government jobs for tribals (Scheduled

Tribes) and Dalits (Scheduled Castes), with the remaining 75% open to all candidates. This arrangement, while not perfect, had seemed reasonably balanced to most students.

However, when the ruling Janata Dal government implemented the Mandal Commission recommendations, mandating 50% reservation, general category students suddenly found half of all education and job vacancies eliminated from contention. Many of us perceived this as a deathblow to meritocracy, a political calculation designed to secure vote banks at the expense of capable students and job seekers who would be denied opportunities solely due to their birth circumstances.

The counterarguments about historical injustices perpetrated by forward castes failed to convince us. We believed such historical wrongs should be addressed through greater political representation at all levels of government rather than through social engineering that compromised merit. We feared—correctly, as it turned out—that this policy would encourage India's most talented students to seek educational and professional opportunities abroad, particularly in the United States and Europe, where they would contribute to those economies rather than to the development of India's domestic research and development capabilities. This brain drain created deficiencies that India continues to struggle with today as we attempt to compete with China's rising technological dominance and Western hegemony.

As student protests erupted across northern India, we found ourselves participating in a political movement for the first time. One day at Ambala, our student union leader urged us to join students from other local colleges in blocking GT Road—the main artery connecting Delhi with Punjab and Kashmir. The experience of halting traffic on this major highway demonstrated the potential power of collective student action, but it also revealed the moral complexities of protest.

Watching stranded passengers growing increasingly uncomfortable and fearful, I questioned whether inconveniencing fellow citizens was an appropriate response to our grievances. Unlike the aggrieved Muslim and "farmer" protesters in Delhi in 2020, who seemed indifferent to public hardship, we decided to abandon our road blockade and return to campus for a sit-in demonstration instead. This decision, while ethically sound, had unforeseen consequences.

That afternoon, political thugs known as the "Chautala Brigade" exploited the chaos created by student protests to commit arson in Ambala city. They set fire to the Life Insurance Corporation building and the Sales Tax office—apparently to destroy evidence of corruption involving their political patrons. To ensure these documents burned completely, they also attacked the fire station, preventing emergency response. When military assistance was requested and an Air Force fire tanker dispatched, the goons intercepted and torched it as well.

This escalation prompted civil authorities to formally request Army intervention. Troops conducted a flag march through the city, announcing shoot-at-sight orders for arsonists, while Section 144 of the Indian Penal Code was imposed, prohibiting gatherings of five or more persons and creating near-curfew conditions. Our legitimate student grievances had been completely overshadowed by violence and political manipulation.

The situation in Delhi proved even more tragic, with authorities firing on unarmed students protesting at India Gate, resulting in multiple deaths. Feeling abandoned and unheard, some students turned to desperate measures. Rajiv Goswami, a Delhi University student, attempted self-immolation at India Gate—an act that, while not fatal in his case, inspired similar protests nationwide. Not all students were as fortunate; one from our own college died after setting herself ablaze.

We organised a candlelight march through Ambala city to honour our fallen classmate, carefully avoiding disrupting traffic by keeping to footpaths and roadsides. The following day, as we gathered on campus for a memorial service, police inexplicably stormed the college grounds and initiated a lathi charge. The five-foot canes with metal-capped tips created panic as students fled, only to discover that police had blocked the exit gates—a terrifying echo of the Jallianwala Bagh massacre during British colonial rule.

With no alternative escape route, students began breaking first-floor classroom windows facing the street and jumping to safety. The police showed no restraint, attacking female students and causing multiple injuries among male students who attempted to protect them. Several classmates suffered fractured hands and heads from the metal-tipped lathis. This brutality shocked me, though my father had described similar police violence during food protests in 1950s Bengal. Witnessing it firsthand in 1990 revealed how little had changed in four decades—the colonial legacy of crowd control through excessive force remained intact despite independence.

The anti-Mandal movement ultimately fizzled out by November 1990, lacking political support and media attention. Classes resumed, and the academic calendar proceeded as though nothing had happened. However, this experience fundamentally altered my understanding of politics, revealing how easily legitimate grievances could be hijacked, how quickly authorities could resort to violence against their own citizens, and how disposable student concerns were in the larger political calculus. These lessons in political realism tempered my youthful idealism and provided context for understanding later social movements throughout my life.

Self-Discovery through Extracurriculars

As the political turmoil subsided and normal university life resumed, I turned my attention to exploring different facets of my personality. Having always enjoyed public speaking but lacking formal training, I joined the college's "Young Speakers' Club" and participated in a one-day workshop on effective communication. Despite previous experience in recitation and elocution competitions during school, I identified significant deficiencies in my posture, voice modulation, and eye contact.

Armed with these newly acquired skills, I entered the college "Talent Show" speech contest—only to receive polite but pointed criticism from judges who noted that I had overemphasised technical elements at the expense of clear message delivery. This feedback, though initially disappointing, proved invaluable for my development as a communicator. I internalised the lesson that technique should serve content rather than overshadow it—a principle that would later help me become an effective presenter and teacher.

Determined to improve, I continued practising and eventually won the college's Extempore Speech contest, an achievement I would repeat twice during my postgraduate studies. The Talent Show wasn't a complete loss either—I won the quiz competition and received a prize of fifty rupees, a substantial sum for a student in 1990.

Drawn by my lifelong affinity for military structure and discipline, I also joined the college's NCC programme. Unlike the Air Wing NCC I had participated in during school, the college offered the Senior Division Army Wing, Infantry Company of the No. 7 Haryana Battalion NCC. This introduced me to Army terminology and practices that differed significantly from Air Force conventions. I learned that "Tiger" meant trigger, "chidiya" referred to the aiming foresight on a rifle barrel, "bay-net" was bayonet, and that during a bayonet charge, one shouted "dhaa-waaaaaa" followed by "ghop-nikaal-ghop-nikaal" in quick succession.

The rifle drill presented new challenges, particularly mastering the complex three-step "salami shastra" with the heavy British World War II-era Lee-Enfield "three-not-three" (.303

calibre) rifle. Marching with the rifle at the "bagal shastra" position proved especially taxing, as the entire weight of the weapon had to be supported by the right middle finger in the trigger guard while keeping the rifle close to the body using the right forearm. When I described this difficulty to my father, he shared a veteran's trick: deceptively using both middle and ring fingers in the trigger guard while balancing the rifle against the body with the index finger and forearm working together.

This advice highlighted the contrast between Air Force and Army equipment—while the Air Force continued using the antiquated "three-not-three" for drills and firing, the Army had upgraded to the FN-FAL 7.62mm rifle with a pistol grip that could be held with a full fist, making parade movements considerably more comfortable.

Range-firing day coincided with the beginning of the 1991 Gulf War—January 17th, when the United States and coalition forces initiated their bombing campaign against Saddam Hussein's Iraq. Like many young Indians at that time, I harboured anti-American sentiments following the Soviet Union's collapse, viewing U.S. military action as hegemonic overreach (regardless of Iraq's earlier annexation of Kuwait). Many Indian military officers had served as instructors and trainers for Iraqi forces, creating additional sympathy for Iraq among Indian defence communities.

Filled with youthful bravado and geopolitical ignorance, my fellow cadets and I attached "I-Love-Saddam" cards to our uniforms and shouted insults at American military leaders while firing our rifles. Looking back, this behaviour seems childish and misguided, but at the time, we considered it a serious political statement.

The range experience itself proved challenging due to my deteriorating eyesight. As a bespectacled cadet with myopic vision, I found that my glasses interfered with proper sight alignment. Removing them created its own problems, as the old-fashioned rifle design positioned the butt against the lower part of my right eye—another issue that wouldn't have occurred with the Army's more modern FN-FAL rifle. Despite these difficulties, I managed to place all ten rounds on target at 100 yards, though none hit the bullseye.

The aspect of Infantry training I most enjoyed was map reading and compass navigation. I developed proficiency in determining positions in unfamiliar terrain and could easily perform "map-to-ground" and "ground-to-map" referencing to chart optimal patrol routes, particularly for night operations. This skill gave me confidence that I would be selected for the NCC Basic Leadership Course at the Rajputana Rifles Regimental Centre in Delhi, potentially competing in navigation events and advancing to the coveted "Para Basic" course at the Paratroopers Training School, Agra. However, as with many youthful ambitions, fate had other plans.

Literary Discoveries and Philosophical Growth

As my interest in English literature blossomed during my first year of college, I achieved the unexpected distinction of topping the subject. The formal study of literature expanded my understanding of literary forms—I learned that "comedy" technically referred to plays with happy endings, while what we colloquially called "comedy" was properly termed "farce." I developed a particular appreciation for the melancholic imagery in John Keats's poetry and the vivid natural descriptions in William Wordsworth's works.

However, the book that most profoundly influenced my worldview during this period wasn't part of the curriculum. Richard Bach's *Jonathan Livingston Seagull* initially attracted me because of its aviation themes—the author being a pilot himself, his descriptions of flight and aerobatic manoeuvres appealed to my lifelong fascination with aircraft. As I read deeper, the narrative transcended physical flight to explore spiritual dimensions and the quest for perfection.

Bach's suggestion that death merely represents a transition to another dimension with fewer limitations resonated with me, offering a philosophical framework that complemented the practical realities I had witnessed growing up in military environments. Years later, in 2019, I revisited this book and discovered Bach had added two chapters that further developed these themes, distinguishing spirituality as a quest for perfection from religiosity with its emphasis on rituals and traditions.

Reading this work made me wish Bach could have encountered Indian spiritual traditions, which—unlike the Abrahamic "religions of the book"—encourage personal exploration and discovery. In Indian spiritual practice, the guru functions more like a doctoral advisor, guiding rather than dictating the seeker's journey. This approach aligned with my evolving understanding of knowledge acquisition and personal growth.

The college library became my sanctuary—a place where ideas could be explored without the immediate practical applications demanded by military life. While the Air Force's existence had always emphasised concrete skills and measurable outcomes, literature offered space for ambiguity, interpretation, and philosophical questioning. This balance between practical capability and intellectual exploration would become a defining characteristic of my approach to life and learning.

Farewell to Ambala: A Journey to the Hills

After completing my first year of college, our family's nomadic military life reasserted itself. My father received transfer orders to the Black Panthers squadron operating MiG-21s at Nal, near Bikaner. This presented a difficult choice: remain alone in Ambala to continue my studies or accompany my parents to their new posting. The decision, though seemingly straightforward, carried significant implications for my academic trajectory and personal development.

Several factors influenced my deliberations. My health had become a concern—I was undergoing treatment for a duodenal ulcer, causing my mother considerable anxiety about my well-being if left unsupervised. Practical financial considerations also weighed heavily. My father's modest salary as a non-commissioned officer couldn't stretch to maintain the family at Bikaner while simultaneously funding my accommodation at the college hostel in Ambala. The mathematics of military pay scales rarely accommodated such divided living arrangements.

"Perhaps you could stay with the Sarkars," my father suggested one evening, referring to a colleague's family who would remain in Ambala. "They've offered to host you until you complete your degree."

The alternative—living with one of my father's colleagues' families—felt uncomfortable, despite their generous offers. I valued privacy and independence too highly to impose on another household, where I would inevitably feel like a guest rather than a family member, constantly mindful of my behaviour and impact on their domestic routines. The prospect of navigating another family's unspoken rules and expectations for two more years seemed more daunting than starting fresh elsewhere.

"I appreciate the offer," I told my father, "...but I think it's better if I come with you and Mother. I can continue my studies somewhere near Bikaner."

He nodded, understanding the unspoken concerns behind my decision. Military children develop acute sensitivity to the dynamics of belonging and displacement; we recognise the difference between being welcomed as a temporary visitor and truly having a place of one's own. Reluctantly, I concluded that my time at S.D. College and in Ambala must end after just one year—another abbreviated chapter in my peripatetic life.

Before departing, my college friend and I embarked on a final adventure—a trip to Shimla, the beautiful hill station just five hours from Ambala by road. This marked my first experience visiting mountainous terrain, having spent my entire life in the plains of northern India. The prospect of seeing the Himalayas, even their foothills, filled me with anticipation that momentarily overshadowed the impending farewell to Ambala.

We arranged accommodation at a wooden guest house belonging to the Khadi Village Industries Commission (KVIC), where my friend's father held a senior position. This connection provided access to lodging that would otherwise have been beyond our student budgets, allowing us to experience Shimla without the financial constraints that typically limited student travel. The guest house, situated on a hillside with panoramic views of the surrounding mountains, promised a perfect base for our exploration.

Our journey encountered an unexpected obstacle when a landslide blocked the road five kilometres from Shimla—a common occurrence during the monsoon season, but one we hadn't anticipated. The bus driver apologetically informed passengers that the road would remain closed for at least twenty-four hours while clearing operations proceeded.

"You can wait here," he advised, "or walk the remaining distance if you're feeling adventurous."

Most passengers chose to return to Chandigarh or find accommodation in nearby villages, but my friend and I, fuelled by youthful enthusiasm and limited time, decided to continue on foot. Undeterred by the prospect of a long walk, we shouldered our backpacks and began trudging from the landslide toward Shimla.

The journey proved more challenging than anticipated. We walked from the landslide to the Shimla bus stand, then climbed the steep incline to the Ridge—the famous open space that serves as Shimla's social hub—before descending via Lakkar Bazar toward our guest house. This became an exhausting trek with our

10-kilogram backpacks, especially challenging given the sudden altitude change from Ambala's 850 feet to Shimla's 7,000 feet elevation.

"I can't believe people live with these inclines every day," I gasped as we paused on a particularly steep section, my legs burning with unaccustomed exertion. "No wonder hill people have such stamina."

My friend, equally winded but determined not to show it, nodded in agreement. "Think of it as preparation for military training," he joked, knowing my background. "Just imagine carrying full combat gear up these slopes."

Despite the physical exertion, the cool mountain breeze revitalised us whenever we paused to catch our breath. The air itself seemed different—lighter, cleaner, infused with the scent of pine and distant snow. Each inhalation felt purifying after the dust and heat of Ambala's plains, providing momentary respite from our burning muscles and aching shoulders.

The architectural landscape of Shimla initially disoriented me—buildings seemingly suspended on hillsides created an unsettling impression of instability, as though the structures might collapse at any moment. Having grown up in the flat military cantonments of northern India, where buildings stood squarely on level ground, I found it difficult to trust these constructions that appeared to defy gravity, clinging to slopes that seemed too steep for permanent habitation.

"How do these buildings not slide down during heavy rains?" I asked my friend, genuinely perplexed by the engineering that allowed multi-storey structures to perch on such precipitous terrain.

"They've been standing for over a century," he replied with the confidence of someone who had visited hill stations before. "The locals know how to build for these conditions."

We spent three unforgettable days exploring Shimla and its surroundings. The experience rendered me uncharacteristically quiet and contemplative, overwhelmed by the majestic scale of the mountains, distant snow-capped Himalayan peaks, hushed forests, and the pervasive greenery. The crisp, clean air created an almost surreal atmosphere that transported me beyond ordinary consciousness.

Our explorations took us along the Mall Road with its colonial-era buildings, to Christ Church with its neo-Gothic architecture, through the winding paths of Jakhu Hill to the famous Hanuman temple, and to the nearby attractions Kufri, Naldehra golf course, Fagu valley, and Wildflower Hall. Each location offered new perspectives on the surrounding landscape, revealing the layered beauty of the mountains from different elevations and angles. The vastness of the panoramas contrasted sharply with the contained horizons of military bases, where perimeter fences and security concerns often limited one's visual field.

Without formally meditating, I found myself in a meditative state, particularly during evenings watching the sunset beyond the valley from our guest house's wooden balcony. As the sun descended behind distant peaks, it transformed the sky into a canvas of extraordinary colours—deep oranges and purples reflecting off scattered clouds, while the mountains themselves turned progressively darker shades of blue and purple as shadows lengthened across their faces.

These moments recalled a Hindi poem I had studied in fourth standard: "Pighlaa Hai Sona Door Gagan Par, Fayl Rahein Hain Shaam Ke Saaye..." (molten gold on the distant sky, spreading shadows of the dusk). The verse, memorised as a classroom exercise years earlier, suddenly acquired vivid meaning as I witnessed the phenomenon it described—the sun's light appearing like liquid gold spilt across the horizon, gradually yielding to evening's advancing shadows.

The natural beauty inspired philosophical reflection on human insignificance against cosmic scales—a humbling perspective that would influence my thinking for years afterwards. Standing before these ancient mountains, formed over millions of years through geological processes of unimaginable power, I felt the transience of human concerns, including my own anxieties about changing colleges and adapting to a new environment. The mountains had witnessed empires rise and fall, yet remained essentially unchanged; they would endure long after my brief existence concluded.

"We're just temporary visitors here," I remarked to my friend during one sunset viewing. "These mountains were ancient before humans existed and will remain long after we're gone."

He nodded thoughtfully. "That's why hill people have a different relationship with time. When you live among these giants, you develop a longer perspective."

Our return journey brought a jarring contrast. As we descended from Shimla's cool elevation toward the plains, the temperature rose steadily, reminding us of the summer heat we had temporarily escaped. By the time we reached Chandigarh, we were sweating profusely, our bodies struggling to readjust to the humidity and heat of lower elevations.

While waiting for our connection to Ambala, I noticed a Hindi newspaper reporting record temperatures in Bikaner, where the Army had recorded 67 degrees Celsius (152.6°F) inside a tank at Mahajan field firing range near my future home. This extreme heat awaited me at my next destination—a dramatic change from Shimla's cool tranquillity. The contrast between these environments could hardly have been more pronounced: from the verdant, misty mountains to the scorched, arid desert; from cool breezes to blistering heat; from lush forests to sparse vegetation.

At that time, I didn't know that this brief mountain sojourn foreshadowed a more significant highland chapter in my life. Within the next decade, the hills would become my abode at a crucial juncture of my life's journey—a future development I could not have anticipated as our bus wound its way back to Ambala's familiar plains.

That night, I departed Ambala, leaving behind the site of my adolescence and early adulthood. My father, mother, younger brother and I boarded the train that would carry us across Punjab toward Bikaner's blazing desert—a new frontier both geographically and personally. As the train pulled away from the platform, I watched Ambala recede into the distance, mentally cataloguing the experiences and growth that had occurred during my time there: my first exposure to civilian education, my political awakening during the anti-Mandal protests, my literary discoveries, and the friendships that had expanded my understanding of life beyond military parameters.

Though my college experience had been abbreviated, it had provided crucial exposure to civilian life, political realities, and intellectual pursuits beyond the structured military environment of my childhood. These lessons would prove valuable as I continued navigating between military and civilian worlds, seeking my own path while carrying forward the values instilled by my Air Force upbringing.

Reflections on My College Awakening

As our train rumbled into the darkness of night, I reflected on the contrasts I had experienced in recent days—from the flooded fields of monsoon-drenched Ambala to the snow-capped peaks visible from Shimla, and now toward the desert heat of Bikaner. These geographical extremes mirrored the transitions occurring within me: from the structured military child to the briefly independent college student, and now toward whatever identity would emerge in the crucible of Rajasthan.

The newspaper with its temperature report lay folded on my lap, a tangible reminder of the challenging environment ahead. Yet alongside apprehension, I felt a growing curiosity about this new chapter. The desert, like the mountains, would have its own lessons to teach—about endurance, adaptation, and finding beauty in seemingly harsh conditions. Little did I know that this desert posting would test not only the resilience my Air Force childhood had instilled but also the independence my brief college experience had nurtured, forging yet another layer of identity in the land of extreme heat, Rajput chivalry, and a folk cultural mosaic.

As the train continued south-westward, I opened my copy of *Jonathan Livingston Seagull*, finding comfort in Bach's words about transcending limitations and discovering new horizons. Perhaps, like Jonathan, I would find unexpected freedom in this next transition, learning to soar in the scorching updrafts of the Rajasthan desert just as I had begun to spread my wings in Ambala's civilian world.

Chapter 5

Desert Chronicles: Finding My Way in Bikaner's Crucible

Journey to the Desert Frontier

Our train journey to Bikaner marked my first real encounter with the Rajasthan desert—a landscape that would become both my challenge and my teacher over the coming years. We travelled in a non-AC first-class coach, with an entire coup to ourselves—my father, mother, younger brother, and me. When we woke on the second morning, the train had halted at Suratgarh Junction station, presenting a scene that immediately captured my attention: dozens of T-72 tanks being unloaded from military train wagons, some already secured on tank trailers ready for transport.

The sight triggered a memory of recent newspaper reports about the Mahajan Field Firing Range between Bikaner and Suratgarh, where the Army had recorded temperatures exceeding 60 degrees Celsius inside its tanks. Yet the morning air felt surprisingly pleasant, almost cool—my first lesson in the desert's deceptive nature and dramatic temperature fluctuations.

As the train pulled away from the station, we eagerly opened the windows, hoping to enjoy the cool desert morning breeze. Instead, we received a harsh introduction to desert reality—our coup instantly filled with fine sand and dust carried by the sudden gust of wind. My mother recoiled in discomfort, brushing frantically at her clothes and hair while trying to shield her eyes from the invasive particles.

"This is terrible!" she exclaimed, quickly moving to close the windows. "How can people live with this constant dust?"

Rather than sharing her distress, I experienced an unexpected reaction—a strange sense of connection with this raw, unfiltered environment. While my family members scrambled to protect themselves from the dust, I simply rolled over on my berth, allowing the fine sand to settle on my clothes, hair, and the two-day stubble on my face.

"Welcome to the desert!" I announced with inexplicable enthusiasm, spreading my arms as though embracing an old friend. My family stared at me with a mixture of confusion and concern, clearly questioning my sanity. Yet I couldn't explain the peculiar sensation of belonging that had suddenly overtaken me—as though some dormant part of my consciousness recognised this harsh landscape as familiar territory.

This feeling of connection with the desert—despite having spent my entire life in the greener, more temperate regions of northern India—would become a recurring theme during my time in Bikaner. Perhaps it stemmed from my military upbringing, which had instilled an adaptability to new environments and a tendency to find beauty in unconventional settings. Or perhaps the desert's stark honesty—its refusal to disguise its harsh realities behind comfortable illusions—resonated with some fundamental aspect of my character.

When we finally reached our destination, I discovered we had arrived not at Bikaner station as expected, but at Lalgarh Junction on the outskirts of the city. The reason soon became apparent: Bikaner station still operated on the narrower metre-gauge tracks, while Lalgarh Junction had been upgraded to broad gauge to accommodate heavier military equipment. This technical detail revealed much about the region's strategic importance.

As we disembarked, the military presence was overwhelming. The platform and surrounding areas teemed with soldiers, military transports, and more tanks. Lalgarh Junction functioned primarily as a logistics hub for the military units stationed in the region, particularly the armoured and mechanised infantry components that required the wider railway gauge for transportation.

"This isn't just any military base," my father explained as we waited for our luggage. "Bikaner hosts the 'Ranbankura' Infantry Division—one of the new RAPID formations."

I would later learn that RAPID—Reorganised Army Plains Infantry Division—represented General K. Sundarji's innovative approach to modern warfare, combining highly mobile armoured and mechanised infantry units with integrated attack helicopter support from the Air Force. These formations were specifically designed to exploit Pakistan's vulnerable north–south axis, applying lessons learned during 'Operation Brass Tacks' that I had witnessed from Ambala four years earlier.

My father had opted for civilian accommodation in Bikaner town rather than quarters at Nal air base, which lay at a considerable distance from the city. This decision would significantly shape my experience, immersing me more deeply in civilian life while maintaining connections to the military community through my father's service. It also meant I would see more of the Army's operations than the Air Force activities that had dominated my childhood landscape—an unexpected shift in my military education.

"You'll be seeing more tanks than aircraft for a change," my father remarked as we loaded our belongings into the transport that would take us to our new home. "Might give you a different perspective on defence operations."

He couldn't have known how prophetic those words would prove, not just in terms of my immediate surroundings but in the broader trajectory of my life. The desert would indeed offer a different perspective—on military service, on academic pursuits, on social structures, and ultimately on my own identity and aspirations.

The Desert's Dual Nature

My first weeks in Bikaner revealed the desert's fascinating contradictions—a landscape of extremes that defied simple categorisation. The daytime heat was truly ferocious, often exceeding 48 degrees Celsius according to official measurements, though my father reported that readings at Nal air base frequently surpassed 50 degrees. This intense heat restricted fighter operations to morning and evening hours, when temperatures became marginally more tolerable for both personnel and equipment.

"Even the Pakistanis across the border must be following similar schedules," I remarked to my father one evening. "Otherwise, we'd be at a serious disadvantage if hostilities ever erupted during the summer months."

"Don't count on it," he replied with the pragmatism of a career serviceman. "Military necessity often overrides comfort considerations. That's why we maintain readiness regardless of conditions."

This observation was confirmed whenever I travelled to the air base for treatment of my ongoing duodenal ulcer. Along the route, I would regularly observe Army units conducting exercises in full desert camouflage despite the punishing midday heat—infantry, armour, artillery, signals, and engineers all training as though temperature were merely an inconvenient detail rather than a potentially lethal environmental factor.

"No wonder Army personnel consider the Air Force a 'fair-weather friend,'" my father once commented with a mixture of amusement and professional pride. "Different services, different operational parameters."

Yet for all its daytime ferocity, the desert offered surprising respite during mornings and evenings, when cool breezes created conditions so pleasant they seemed to belong to an entirely different climate. Most remarkable were the nights, when temperatures plummeted to levels requiring not just blankets but quilts for comfort—a dramatic swing that continually astonished me despite intellectual understanding of desert thermodynamics.

We adapted to this rhythm by sleeping on the roof terrace of our rented accommodation, escaping the stifling heat trapped within rooms that had absorbed solar radiation throughout the day. These nights under the vast desert sky, with stars so close they seemed to touch in the clear, dry air, became one of my most treasured experiences in Bikaner. The silence of the desert night, broken only by occasional distant sounds from the city or military vehicles on night exercises, created perfect conditions for contemplation and introspection.

The desert's visual palette proved equally striking. Contrary to popular imagination of deserts as monotonous expanses of beige sand, Bikaner's landscape displayed remarkable chromatic range, particularly during transition hours. Dawn and dusk transformed the environment with pink and orange hues that suffused both land and sky. The setting sun, unobstructed by vegetation or topographical features, bathed everything in a golden light reminiscent of the "molten gold" I had witnessed in Shimla's mountains just weeks earlier—a surprising parallel between environments I had assumed would have nothing in common.

This observation reinforced my growing appreciation for nature's continuities across seemingly disparate landscapes. The same sun that gilded Himalayan peaks also illuminated desert dunes; the same stars overlooked both environments with equal indifference to human concerns. This perspective helped me maintain a connection with my brief mountain experience while adapting to radically different surroundings.

The desert's harshness occasionally manifested in unexpected ways. One afternoon, while installing a television antenna on our roof in the blistering heat, wearing only shorts, I felt an unusual burning sensation across my exposed back. Upon returning indoors, my mother noticed small blisters forming on my skin—actual thermal burns caused by direct sun exposure for less than thirty minutes. This incident provided a visceral understanding of why desert dwellers traditionally covered their bodies completely despite the heat, prioritising protection from solar radiation over momentary comfort.

Beyond these physical characteristics, the desert environment shaped military operations in ways that fascinated my strategically inclined mind. Both Indian and Pakistani air forces engaged in routine "cat-and-mouse" games along the border, testing each other's reaction times and surveillance capabilities. My father and his colleagues would often discuss sudden scrambles by the "Black Panthers" squadron's MiG-21s to intercept "bogies" detected by Bikaner's airspace surveillance radar.

These conversations sometimes included mentions of intelligence gathered through eavesdropping on Pakistani radio communications, facilitated by the massive tropospheric scatter antennas—affectionately called "tropo" in Air Force parlance—visible from miles away as twin "rabbit ears" at Nal air base. These technical details fascinated me, offering glimpses into the sophisticated electronic warfare and surveillance operations that complemented more visible military activities.

"It's all very exciting during peacetime," a senior officer once remarked during a social gathering at our home. "But everyone understands how quickly these games could become deadly serious with just one miscalculation or moment of overconfidence—whether by pilots or SAM (surface-to-air missile) crews on either side."

This observation underscored the perpetual tension along the border—a situation that appeared routine and almost recreational to casual observers but contained potential for rapid escalation that military professionals never forgot. The desert's vast openness, which allowed unobstructed observation of adversary movements, paradoxically increased both transparency and suspicion, creating a unique operational environment unlike the mountainous northern borders or the naval frontier to the south.

Living in this environment, I developed a heightened awareness of geopolitical realities that textbooks could never fully convey. The proximity to Pakistan—just minutes of flying time away—made international relations tangible rather than theoretical. Border tensions weren't abstract concepts but daily realities reflected in aircraft movements, radar activations, and the constant vigilance of personnel stationed along the frontier.

This immersion in strategic geography would significantly influence my worldview, reinforcing my interest in international affairs while providing a practical context for understanding defence policies and military deployments. The desert, far from being an empty wasteland, revealed itself as a complex operational theatre where geography, technology, and human factors intersected in constantly evolving patterns of deterrence and preparation.

Academic Setbacks and Unexpected Opportunities

My transition to Bikaner's educational system proved more challenging than anticipated, beginning with a significant academic setback. Upon approaching Rampuria College—one of only two degree colleges in Bikaner at that time—I discovered that transferring mid-programme between different university systems was not straightforward. The principal explained that partial degrees from different universities were not recognised, meaning I would need to restart from first year, despite having completed one year at S.D. College in Ambala.

This news was disappointing enough, but further complications arose regarding subject selection. The Economics department had reached its enrolment capacity, forcing me to substitute History for my preferred discipline. While I maintained English Literature and Political Science from my previous programme, losing Economics—a subject that had increasingly captured my intellectual interest—felt like a significant sacrifice.

"I understand your disappointment," the principal said with genuine sympathy, "but perhaps History will prove valuable, given your interest in military affairs and international relations. After all, strategy without historical context is merely a tactical reaction."

His perspective helped me rationalise the change, though it didn't entirely alleviate my frustration. I had developed a genuine passion for economic theory during my year at S.D. College, particularly in macroeconomic policy and development economics. Being forced to abandon this intellectual trajectory due to administrative constraints rather than personal choice felt arbitrary and unfair.

Another disappointment awaited when I attempted to join the college's NCC programme, hoping to continue the military training I had valued so highly in Ambala. To my dismay, I was informed that my height—just *5'3"*—disqualified me from participation in Rajasthan NCC units, which apparently prioritised physical stature for their marching contingents.

"We focus primarily on drill and ceremonial functions," the NCC officer explained, without apparent concern for my evident disappointment. "Candidates must meet minimum height requirements for visual uniformity during parades and public displays."

This explanation struck me as absurdly superficial, particularly given my previous positive experience with Haryana's NCC battalion, which had valued diverse military skills, including map-reading and compass navigation, rather than merely ceremonial appearance. The rejection felt like the final nail in the coffin of my military aspirations, confirming that physical characteristics beyond my control would forever limit my participation in the profession that had shaped my identity since childhood.

The college environment itself presented additional challenges, unlike the relatively cosmopolitan atmosphere of military schools and S.D. College, Rampuria College operated within rigid social hierarchies based on caste and religious identity. Students self-segregated into distinct groups—Rajputs (locally called "Bannaa"), Brahmins, and Muslims—maintaining separate social circles, eating arrangements, and extracurricular activities.

As a newcomer with a military background and Bengali heritage, I occupied an ambiguous position within this social ecosystem. Brahmin students welcomed me based on shared caste identity, while Rajputs showed interest in my military connections. Muslim students generally maintained distance, though whether from preference or perceived social expectations remained unclear.

Rather than challenging these divisions, I adopted a pragmatic approach—interacting respectfully with all groups while avoiding judgement of local social customs. "Who am I, as an 'outsider,' to question the way people have lived and thought for generations?" I reasoned. "Any meaningful social change must develop organically rather than through external imposition."

This perspective—that cultural evolution should proceed from within communities rather than through external pressure—would influence my thinking throughout life, particularly regarding development work and social interventions. I had studied enough history to recognise the devastating consequences when external powers imposed their values on indigenous populations, as European colonisers had done to Native American and African cultures. This awareness made me deeply sceptical of top-down approaches to social change, regardless of how well-intentioned they might appear.

Approximately two months into the academic year, an unexpected opportunity arose when the principal summoned me to his office. "I've reviewed your case more thoroughly," he announced, "and determined that you qualify for direct admission to the second year. Furthermore, we can accommodate you in the Economics department after all, replacing History in your subject combination."

This news initially seemed miraculous—I would recover the year I thought lost and resume studying my preferred subject. Only much later would I understand the administrative peculiarity that made this possible: Rajasthan had operated on a 10+1+3 educational system (ten years of primary/secondary school, one year of higher secondary, and three years of undergraduate study) until 1991, when it transitioned to the 10+2+3 system used throughout most of India.

Having completed twelve years of schooling before college, I qualified for direct entry into the second year under the old system, effectively creating a 10+2+2 pattern for my undergraduate education. While this arrangement saved me a year of study, it would later create complications for advanced degree programmes that specifically required the standard 10+2+3 pattern—a detail that seemed inconsequential at the time but would prove significant for my future academic aspirations.

Despite these challenges, I gradually adapted to Rampuria College's academic environment, finding intellectual stimulation in my coursework and developing an appreciation for the diverse teaching approaches of Rajasthani professors compared to those in Haryana. The emphasis on memorisation and textual fidelity initially frustrated me after experiencing more discussion-based learning at S.D. College, but I eventually recognised the value in mastering foundational content before attempting critical analysis.

"First know what the great thinkers have said," my Political Science professor advised, "then you earn the right to question their conclusions."

This methodical approach to knowledge acquisition, while sometimes tedious, provided solid grounding in classical texts and theoretical frameworks that would serve me well in later academic pursuits. By embracing rather than resisting the local educational culture, I discovered valuable complementary perspectives to the more freewheeling intellectual environment I had briefly experienced in Ambala.

Forging New Friendships in Foreign Territory

My social integration into Bikaner's student community progressed through two significant friendships that represented different aspects of local culture. The first was developed with the principal's son, who coincidentally studied in the same second-year programme with identical subjects. His relatively privileged background and exposure to influences beyond Bikaner made him unusually cosmopolitan by local standards, providing a bridge between my previous experiences and the more conservative environment I now inhabited.

"You're not going to believe what I've got," he announced one afternoon, producing cassette tapes of Michael Bolton and Bruce Springsteen albums—Western music that rarely circulated among Bikaner's student population. "My sister brought these back from her MBA programme. They're playing this stuff at all the campus parties."

These musical introductions expanded my cultural horizons beyond Bollywood soundtracks and classical Indian music that had dominated my previous listening. The narrative quality of Springsteen's lyrics particularly resonated with me, offering perspectives on working-class struggles and aspirations that seemed simultaneously foreign and familiar—different in specific cultural references but universal in emotional content.

Our friendship included academic collaboration and social adventures, including occasional class-skipping expeditions to Suraj Talkies, Bikaner's most luxurious cinema. This theatre represented local opulence, featuring small decorative water fountains in the lobby, interiors styled after Rajput palaces, and subtle perfumes sprayed throughout the venue to enhance the sensory experience.

One particularly memorable outing involved watching "Prahaar," a film about Indian Army commando training that naturally appealed to my military interests. The movie featured a scene where the protagonist plans a hostage rescue operation alongside "Colonel Singh"—a character I assumed was fictional until years later, when I realised he was actually Colonel (later General) V.K. Singh, a Rajput Regiment officer who would eventually serve as Chief of Army Staff.

Another significant film experience was "Jo Jeeta Wohi Sikandar," whose theme song—"Vo Sikandar Hi, Doston, Kahalaataa Hai; Haari Baazi Ko Jeetana Jisey Aata Hai..." (He is called Alexander, friends, who knows how to win a lost game)—resonated deeply with my determination to succeed despite the limitations of being a "Rampurian," a label that carried negative connotations in Bikaner's social hierarchy—no girl in Bikaner would like to talk to a "Rampurian".

My friend's Luna moped provided another dimension to our adventures, offering mobility beyond what my Hero Ranger bicycle could achieve. Though my father's modest Air Force salary couldn't stretch to purchasing motorised transportation, these shared rides around Bikaner allowed me to experience the city more extensively than would otherwise have been possible. The sensation of "speed" and relative comfort compared to cycling across sandy terrain made these excursions particularly enjoyable, creating memories of freedom and exploration that balanced the constraints of academic responsibilities.

My second significant friendship developed with a classmate who represented a completely different aspect of Bikaner society. Coming from a conservative Marwari Brahmin family, he embodied local traditions in his appearance and habits—speaking primarily Marwari and Hindi, with minimal English; typically dressed in casual attire with shirts untucked; and habitually chewing gutka (a form of chewing tobacco). Despite these outward markers of traditional identity, he possessed remarkable intellectual curiosity and progressive thinking that transcended his conservative upbringing.

Our conversations frequently explored global affairs and philosophical questions, revealing his sophisticated understanding of international relations despite limited formal exposure to these topics. His perspectives challenged my assumptions about the relationship between educational background and intellectual capacity, demonstrating how innate curiosity and critical thinking could flourish even without access to privileged educational resources.

"People think because I don't speak English well, I don't have thoughts about the world," he once remarked during a particularly engaging discussion about post-Soviet geopolitics. "But understanding doesn't always need fancy words."

His family welcomed me with extraordinary warmth, particularly his mother, who treated me as another son rather than a visitor. Their home became a second residence for me, including occasional overnight stays in the underground cellar—a traditional architectural feature in many Marwari houses designed to provide relief from Bikaner's extreme temperatures. These subterranean rooms maintained remarkably cool conditions even during the hottest days, demonstrating indigenous architectural solutions to environmental challenges long before modern air conditioning.

These visits introduced me to authentic Marwari cuisine—aloo curry, gutta curry, bhujia ki sabji, and chapati, all prepared with generous quantities of ghee, red chilli, and oil. The spice levels initially shocked my system, accustomed to the more moderate seasoning of Bengali cooking, but I quickly developed an appreciation for these robust flavours. My mother expressed concern about potential digestive consequences, but I rarely experienced discomfort despite the dramatic difference from our home cooking.

This culinary adaptation taught me an important lesson about cultural practices and environmental adaptation. The heavy use of spices and oils in Rajasthani cuisine wasn't arbitrary but had evolved specifically to address the challenges of desert living—providing necessary calories for energy in a demanding climate, incorporating preservative elements in a region where food spoilage occurred rapidly, and inducing perspiration to aid the body's cooling mechanisms.

"When in Rome, do as the Romans do," I concluded, recognising that local customs typically represented generations of practical wisdom rather than arbitrary traditions. This insight developed into a lifelong approach to cultural differences—seeking to understand underlying rationales rather than making superficial judgements based on my own cultural references. This perspective would later inform my adventurous approach to international cuisines during global travels, approaching unfamiliar foods with curiosity rather than apprehension.

These complementary friendships—one connecting me to more cosmopolitan influences, the other grounding me in local traditions—created a balanced social experience that facilitated my integration into Bikaner society while maintaining connections to broader cultural currents. Together, they represented the dual nature of my identity during this period: simultaneously adapting to local conditions while maintaining awareness of perspectives beyond immediate surroundings.

Military Connections in Civilian Territory

Despite my predominantly civilian existence in Bikaner, military influences remained significant through my father's service and occasional visits to Nal Air Base. These connections maintained my sense of belonging to the defence community even as I navigated civilian educational and social environments, creating a dual identity that sometimes generated cognitive dissonance but ultimately enriched my perspective.

Evening gatherings at my father's colleagues' homes provided regular updates on Air Force operations, particularly the ongoing "cat-and-mouse" activities between Indian and Pakistani air forces along the border. These conversations offered fascinating glimpses into operational realities that rarely appeared in news reports or academic discussions of international relations. The matter-of-fact descriptions of interceptor scrambles, radar tracking, and electronic intelligence gathering revealed the constant vigilance maintained even during nominal peacetime—a parallel reality operating alongside civilian life but largely invisible to those outside military circles.

Occasional visits to Nal Air Base in Air Force "Shaktimaan" trucks reinforced my connection to this world. One particularly memorable occasion was the year-end party on December 31, 1992, at the Senior Non-Commissioned Officers' (SNCOs') Mess. The event followed familiar patterns from my Ambala experiences—Tambola games, Bollywood movie screenings on video, and elaborate buffet meals described as "Badaa Khaanaa" in military parlance—creating a comforting sense of continuity with previous postings despite the different geographical setting.

The evening included an unexpected interaction when Group Captain Dhillon, the Station Commander, made an appearance to extend New Year wishes to the SNCOs and their families. As he moved through the gathering, shaking hands, he paused upon reaching me, commenting with amusement, "Nowadays we are getting pretty young SNCOs!"

His remark referenced my instinctive military bearing—crew-cut hair, ramrod-straight posture, firm handshake, and crisp "Sir!" acknowledgement—behaviours so deeply ingrained through my upbringing that they manifested automatically in appropriate contexts. The officer's observation, though light-hearted, affirmed my self-perception as a "natural soldier" in demeanour and mindset despite my civilian status.

This incident crystallised the duality of my identity during this period—formally a civilian student but fundamentally shaped by military culture and values. My automatic adoption of military protocols in the presence of a senior officer reflected not conscious performance but genuine internalisation of the defence forces' ethos through years of immersion in that environment. Despite my civilian clothes and student status, I remained recognisably military in fundamental aspects of self-presentation and interaction.

This duality occasionally created challenges in civilian contexts, where my military-influenced behaviours sometimes appeared excessively formal or rigid to classmates and professors accustomed to more relaxed social norms. Conversely, my growing comfort with civilian independence and intellectual exploration sometimes felt discordant with the structured hierarchies and operational focus of military environments. Navigating these different behavioural expectations required conscious code-switching between contexts—a skill that would prove valuable throughout my later career, spanning multiple professional cultures.

The military influence extended beyond personal behaviour to my understanding of regional geography and strategic considerations. Living near the western border provided concrete appreciation of concepts that had previously existed primarily as abstract knowledge—the significance of reaction times in aerial interception, the importance of early warning systems, the logistical challenges of desert operations, and the psychological dimensions of deterrence through visible preparation.

Observing Army exercises in the surrounding desert areas complemented my Air Force background, offering insights into ground operations that had previously been peripheral to my understanding of military affairs. The tanks and armoured personnel carriers manoeuvring across sandy terrain, artillery units establishing firing positions, and infantry conducting desert warfare drills all expanded my comprehension of joint operations and the distinct challenges faced by different service branches in desert environments.

These observations proved particularly valuable given my lifelong interest in military strategy and operations. While my formal education increasingly focused on economics and political science, these firsthand exposures to defence activities provided complementary knowledge that textbooks could never fully convey. The integration of academic concepts with observed realities created a more sophisticated understanding of security issues than either approach could have provided in isolation.

This period also coincided with significant international developments that influenced military thinking and operations. The 1991 Gulf War demonstrated the decisive impact of air power and precision munitions in desert warfare, while the Soviet Union's collapse transformed global security architectures that had remained relatively stable for decades. These events generated extensive discussion within military circles, providing me with indirect exposure to professional analyses of changing strategic paradigms.

My position at the intersection of military and civilian worlds during this formative period would significantly influence my later approach to professional challenges and organisational cultures. The ability to understand both military precision and civilian flexibility, hierarchical efficiency and democratic deliberation, operational focus and theoretical exploration—these dual perspectives would later prove valuable in navigating complex institutional environments and building bridges between different professional communities.

Cultural Immersion and Identity Formation

Bikaner's distinctive cultural landscape provided rich opportunities for personal growth and identity exploration during my late teenage years. The city's heritage as a former princely state had created unique social structures and cultural expressions that differed significantly from both my Bengali family background and the somewhat homogenised military community environment of my childhood.

The most immediately striking aspect of local culture was the rigid caste consciousness that permeated social interactions. Unlike the relatively fluid social environment of military bases, where rank rather than birth determined status and where diverse regional and religious backgrounds coexisted with minimal friction, Bikaner society maintained clear demarcations between different communities. These divisions manifested not just in major life decisions like marriage and career selection but in everyday interactions—friendship groups, dining arrangements, and even casual conversations.

As an outsider with complex identity markers—Bengali by ethnicity, Brahmin by caste, military by upbringing, but without local family connections—I occupied an ambiguous position within this social ecosystem. This liminality sometimes created awkward situations but also afforded unique opportunities for observation and interaction across boundaries that locals rarely crossed.

"You're not really from anywhere, are you?" a classmate once remarked, intending the observation as a simple fact rather than criticism. "That must make it easier to talk to everyone without worrying about what people will think."

His assessment contained significant truth. My status as a perpetual outsider—first as a military child moving between postings, now as a Bengali in Rajasthan—had cultivated adaptability and observational skills that served me well in navigating unfamiliar social terrain. Rather than attempting to assimilate completely into any single community, I developed the ability to understand and respect diverse perspectives while maintaining my own distinct identity.

This approach allowed me to appreciate Bikaner's rich cultural heritage without feeling pressured to adopt all its conventions. I could admire the architectural splendour of the Rampuria havelis—elaborate mansions built by wealthy Marwari merchants featuring intricate stone carving and distinctive architectural elements—while simultaneously recognising the economic disparities they represented. I could respect the deep religious devotion evident in local practices while maintaining my own more philosophical approach to spiritual questions.

The conservative social attitudes prevalent in Bikaner, particularly regarding gender roles and interactions, presented occasional challenges to my more progressive inclinations. Rampuria College's predominantly male student body and the evident discomfort many students displayed around women reflected patriarchal traditions that contrasted sharply with the relatively egalitarian environment of military communities, where women's contributions were generally valued and respected.

This contrast became particularly apparent when comparing Rampuria College with Dungar College, the city's other major educational institution. While Rampuria remained largely single-gender in practice if not policy, with few female students and those present maintaining extremely limited social interactions, Dungar College operated as a genuinely co-educational environment where male and female students interacted more freely. This difference reflected broader social divisions between traditional and modernising segments of Bikaner society.

"No girl in Bikaner would want to talk to a Rampurian" became a common refrain among my classmates, acknowledging the negative reputation our institution had acquired regarding the treatment of women. While I found this generalisation unfair to many respectful students, I couldn't deny the problematic behaviours I occasionally witnessed—inappropriate comments, uncomfortable staring, and general awkwardness that created unwelcoming environments for female students and visitors.

Rather than simply accepting or rejecting local cultural norms wholesale, I attempted to develop a nuanced understanding of their origins and functions. Many practices that initially appeared arbitrary or regressive revealed underlying rationales when examined in a historical and environmental context. The conservative dress codes that seemed restrictive by contemporary standards had evolved as practical adaptations to desert conditions, protecting skin from harsh sun and blowing sand. Dietary restrictions often reflected food-preservation challenges in pre-refrigeration desert environments. Even social hierarchies, while problematic from egalitarian perspectives, had provided organisational stability during historical periods of resource scarcity and external threat.

This contextual understanding didn't justify perpetuating harmful or discriminatory practices but did foster appreciation for the complex evolutionary processes that had shaped local culture. Rather than dismissing traditions as simply backward or irrational, I learned to identify the original adaptive functions they had served while still advocating for modifications that addressed contemporary ethical concerns and changing circumstances.

This balanced perspective—respecting cultural heritage while supporting positive evolution—would inform my later professional approach to development work, where simplistic impositions of external values often created resistance rather than constructive change. The recognition that sustainable social development must build upon existing cultural foundations rather than attempting to replace them entirely became a core principle in my understanding of effective community engagement.

My time in Bikaner also deepened my appreciation for the relationship between environment and culture. The desert's extreme conditions had shaped every aspect of local life—architecture designed to maximise cooling, cuisine developed to address nutritional needs in arid conditions, social structures organised to manage scarce resources, and even artistic expressions reflecting the stark beauty and dramatic light of desert landscapes.

This recognition of environmental influence on cultural development reinforced my growing interest in ecological economics—understanding economic systems as embedded within and constrained by natural systems rather than operating independently from them. While this perspective wasn't explicitly articulated in my undergraduate economics curriculum, the lived experience of desert adaptation provided an intuitive understanding of these relationships that would later connect with formal theoretical frameworks.

The desert itself became a powerful teacher during this period, its extreme conditions stripping away pretensions and revealing essential priorities. When temperatures exceeded 50 degrees Celsius, abstract concerns quickly yielded to immediate physical realities—the vital importance of water conservation, the necessity of mutual aid during environmental challenges, the wisdom of traditional practices developed through generations of desert living. These lessons in practical resilience complemented my academic education, providing experiential knowledge that textbooks could never fully convey.

The Pivotal Decision: Military Service or Management Education

As I approached completion of my undergraduate studies, the question of career direction became increasingly urgent. Two distinct paths had emerged as viable options, each representing different aspects of my identity and interests: military service through the Army's Short Service Commission, or management education leading to corporate career opportunities.

The military option retained powerful appeal, symbolising the continuation of family tradition and alignment with values that had shaped my character since childhood. Despite previous disappointments with NCC height requirements and unsuccessful National Defence Academy applications, the Combined Defence Services Examination offered another potential entry point into military life. This path would fulfil my longstanding desire to serve in uniform, applying the mindset and skills I had absorbed through years of proximity to military culture.

The management path represented newer interests developed during my college years, particularly my growing passion for economics and finance. This direction promised financial stability, professional growth opportunities, and potential escape from the nomadic lifestyle that had characterised my childhood. An MBA from a respected institution could provide entry into corporate environments where analytical abilities and strategic thinking—skills I had developed through both military exposure and academic study—would be valued and rewarded.

With a characteristic methodical approach, I pursued both options simultaneously to maximise future flexibility. I appeared for several MBA entrance examinations while also taking the Combined Defence Services Examination conducted by the Union Public Service Commission. Having learned from previous experience that mathematics was my weakness in earlier military entrance tests, I strategically opted for the Short Service Commission (58th SSC course at the Officers Training Academy,

Chennai), which required testing only in General Knowledge and English—subjects where my strengths lay.

The results arrived in quick succession: acceptance into the MBA programme at the Institute of Management Studies (IMS) Bikaner, followed shortly by notification that I had cleared the CDSE and would be called for the week-long Services Selection Board interview in Allahabad (now Prayagraj). This apparent success on both fronts created an unexpected dilemma—the interview dates for both opportunities conflicted, forcing a definitive choice between the paths rather than further delaying the decision.

This moment represented a genuine crossroads in my life trajectory, with each option offering distinct advantages and limitations. The military path aligned with my ingrained values and identity, but offered modest financial compensation and continued geographical instability. The management path promised economic advancement and settlement but would require adaptation to corporate culture and values that remained largely unfamiliar.

Facing this consequential decision, I sought counsel from my father, whose perspective had always provided reliable guidance during previous life transitions. His advice proved uncharacteristically direct and pragmatic, focusing primarily on material considerations rather than idealistic factors.

"The armed forces don't pay well," he explained with the frankness of someone who had experienced these limitations firsthand. "An officer earns significantly less than a corporate professional of equivalent responsibility and education. And the nomadic lifestyle—constantly relocating with each new posting—drains whatever modest savings you manage to accumulate."

He continued with increasing conviction: "A corporate career after MBA would not only provide welcome stability but help us finally escape the lower middle-class circumstances we've endured. This could be your opportunity to achieve the social and financial status that military service rarely permits."

His perspective reflected genuine concern for my future welfare rather than dismissal of military values. Having dedicated his own career to Air Force service, he understood intimately both the rewards and sacrifices involved—the pride of national service balanced against material limitations and family disruptions. His advice stemmed from a desire to see me achieve greater financial security than he had managed despite decades of dedicated service.

After careful consideration, I accepted his reasoning and decided to pursue the MBA opportunity, declining the SSB interview that might have led to a military commission. This choice represented practical acceptance of economic realities over emotional attachment to military identity—a rational decision that nevertheless carried significant psychological impact.

"This is one moment of my life that I would really like to change," I would often reflect in later years, feeling the persistent pull of the military path not taken. Despite achieving professional success and financial stability through my career, the decision to forgo the Services Selection Board interview remained a source of lingering regret—a road not travelled whose possibilities continued to haunt my imagination.

During my interview at the Institute of Management Studies, I found myself mentally rehearsing what I would have told the SSB interviewing officer about my motivation for joining the Army: "I want to be part of an organisation where people live and die for something unfathomable in civilian life—for 'Naam, Namak aur Nishan' (Honour, Loyalty, and the Colours of the Flag)." These words, though never spoken in their intended context, encapsulated the values that remained central to my identity despite my civilian career trajectory.

Reflections on My Desert Chronicles

The full name of my new academic home—Bahadurmal Jaskaran Sidhkaran Rampuria Jain Mahavidyalaya, commonly shortened to BJS Rampuria College—reflected its origins as a charitable endowment from a prominent Marwari business family. The college's reputation within Bikaner society became apparent through the common refrain that "no girl in Bikaner would like to talk to a Rampurian."

"I was determined to 'make it big' despite being a 'Rampurian,'" I resolved, refusing to accept that institutional reputation should limit personal ambition. This determination found reinforcement in unexpected places, including the inspirational lyrics from *Jo Jeeta Wohi Sikandar*, which became something of a personal anthem during this period: "Vo Sikandar Hee, Doston, Kahalaata Hai; Haaree Baazee Ko Jeetana Jise Aata Hai…" (He is called Alexander, friends, who knows how to turn a losing game into victory).

My decision to pursue management education rather than military service represented not the abandonment of military values but their translation into a civilian context. The discipline, strategic thinking, and leadership principles instilled through my Air Force upbringing would prove valuable assets in corporate environments, though applied toward different objectives. The analytical frameworks I had developed through observing military operations would inform my approach to business challenges, while the adaptability cultivated through frequent relocations would facilitate navigation of changing market conditions and organisational structures.

Nevertheless, the transition from a military-adjacent identity to a civilian professional identity required significant psychological adjustment. Having oriented my self-concept around military values and aspirations since childhood, embracing an alternative path necessitated a fundamental reconsideration of how I defined success and purpose. This process would continue throughout my management education and early professional career, gradually integrating military-derived principles with civilian applications to create a coherent personal and professional identity.

The desert environment that had initially seemed so alien upon arrival had, over time, become a familiar landscape whose extremes and contradictions I had learned to appreciate. The blistering daytime heat, balanced by cool nights; the stark visual beauty of sand dunes illuminated by sunrise and sunset; the resilient communities that had adapted to challenging conditions through ingenious cultural and architectural innovations—these elements had transformed my understanding of adaptation and resilience in ways that would inform my approach to future challenges.

As I prepared for the next phase of my education, I recognised that the desert had shaped me in subtle and profound ways. Beyond specific knowledge or skills, my time in this extreme environment has cultivated a deeper appreciation for contextual understanding, cultural adaptation, and the beauty of unconventional settings. These perspectives would prove valuable throughout my subsequent career, informing my approach to international development work and cross-cultural engagement.

The military presence that had initially drawn my attention upon arrival—the tanks at Suratgarh station, the RAPID division's operations, the border surveillance activities—had provided a continuing connection to defence affairs even as my personal trajectory diverged from military service. This exposure had deepened my understanding of national security considerations while simultaneously highlighting the economic and personal sacrifices made by service members and their families—knowledge that would inform my later professional engagement with defence-related policy issues.

My Bikaner experience had also reinforced my appreciation for the relationship between environment and human systems—how geography, climate, and resource availability shape economic activities, social structures, and cultural practices. This ecological perspective would later connect with formal theoretical frameworks in development economics and sustainable development, providing an experiential foundation for academic concepts encountered during advanced studies.

As I continued my journey toward new educational and professional horizons, I gazed out at the desert landscape with mixed emotions—gratitude for lessons learned, appreciation for friendships formed, and curiosity about how this chapter would influence future developments. The desert had initially appeared merely as a challenging environment to endure. Still, it had revealed itself as a profound teacher whose lessons extended far beyond survival techniques to encompass a deeper understanding of adaptation, resilience, and the meaning of challenging circumstances.

Though my path had diverged from military service, the values instilled through my Air Force childhood and reinforced through proximity to defence operations in Bikaner would remain foundational to my identity and approach to life's challenges. The decision to pursue management education represented not the rejection of these values but their translation into a different context—applying strategic thinking, disciplined execution, and commitment to excellence toward economic and social development rather than national defence.

The desert chapter of my life was closing, but its influence would continue to shape my perspective and decisions through subsequent phases of personal and professional development. Bikaner had not merely been a geographical location but a crucible of identity formation—a place where the heat of circumstance had forged a stronger, more adaptable character capable of finding opportunity in adversity and beauty in starkness. These qualities would serve me well in the professional world that awaited beyond the desert horizon.

Chapter 6

Dust to Destiny: Navigating Life's Crossroads in the Desert

The Unexpected Academic Detour

My journey through the desert landscape of Bikaner continued with an unexpected academic twist that would ultimately reshape my professional trajectory. Having completed my undergraduate studies at Rampuria College with what I believed was a modest but sufficient academic record, I found myself at another crossroads—one that would test not only my intellectual capabilities but also my resilience in navigating bureaucratic labyrinths that seemed determined to impede my progress.

The transition from undergraduate studies to professional education began with a familiar administrative nightmare. The minimum qualifying mark for MBA admission was 50% in graduation, a threshold I had presumably cleared, though just barely. However, as the final moment for document verification arrived, the university had not yet announced the official results—a peculiar situation given that admissions to the university's own MBA programme were already underway.

"How can you accept applications when you haven't even released the results?" I asked the clerk at the administration office, who responded with the practised indifference of someone who had heard this question countless times before.

"Provisional results can be arranged," he replied without looking up from his paperwork. "But you'll need to submit them before the interview process concludes."

This bureaucratic paradox—needing results that hadn't been released to apply for a programme already accepting applications—exemplified the administrative absurdities that often characterised Indian higher education. Fortunately, my friend from Rampuria College, whose connections extended into the university administration at Ajmer, offered assistance that proved invaluable.

"You focus on the Group Discussion and Personal Interview," he advised. "I'll arrange for your provisional result to be ready by tomorrow."

With this arrangement in place, I proceeded to the selection process for the Institute of Management Studies (IMS) Bikaner, an institution that, while perhaps not nationally renowned, held considerable prestige within Rajasthan. The Group Discussion proved unexpectedly orderly—almost suspiciously so. Before entering the examination room, my fellow candidates and I had agreed to a structured approach: we would each speak in turn, presenting our points sequentially before conducting a second round for summaries and rebuttals.

This carefully choreographed performance quickly aroused the examiners' suspicion. Midway through our first round of statements, one panellist interrupted with evident frustration.

"This isn't how group discussions work in real corporate settings," he observed dryly. "Who can summarise what we've heard so far?"

The sudden deviation from our planned approach created momentary confusion among the candidates. No one had prepared to summarise at this juncture, and the silence stretched uncomfortably as we exchanged uncertain glances. Drawing on instincts developed through years of NCC training—where adaptability to changing circumstances was essential—I found myself stepping into the void.

"If I may," I began, summarising the key points raised thus far before inviting others to add perspectives I might have missed. This spontaneous leadership moment, while seemingly minor, reflected the first aim of NCC training that had been instilled in me years earlier: "Development of leadership, character, comradeship, spirit of sportsmanship and ideals of service."

The Personal Interview that followed explored my understanding of management education itself. When asked whether I considered an MBA a form of education or training, I offered a perspective that bridged theoretical foundations with practical applications.

"Education provides conceptual frameworks and analytical tools," I explained, "while training develops specific skills for immediate application. MBA represents the integration of both theoretical understanding and practical decision-making. Without robust theory, practice becomes mere trial and error; without practical application, theory remains abstract and untested."

The final question—why I wanted to pursue an MBA—elicited a response that seemed idealistic even to my own ears: "I want to live in an India that is a developed country, not a developing one. Rather than passively inheriting this 'developed' status, I want to actively contribute to making it happen."

Little did I realise that decades later, "Viksit Bharat 2047" (Developed India 2047) would emerge as a national mission aimed at transforming India into a developed nation by its centenary of independence—a vision that would eventually align with my professional endeavours in ways I couldn't have imagined during that interview.

My friend returned that evening with a sealed envelope containing my provisional results, which I submitted to the selection committee the following day. By midday, the list of thirty successful candidates was announced, with my name appearing at twenty-second position—a placement that surprised even the principal of Rampuria College, who had privately informed my friend that I had barely achieved the minimum 50% requirement.

"One mark less," he had commented, "and you wouldn't have qualified for consideration."

My relatively low position on the merit list, despite strong performance in the aptitude test, group discussion, and personal interview, reflected the weight given to undergraduate academic performance, where other candidates had typically scored above 60%. Nevertheless, I had secured admission to the MBA programme, seemingly overcoming the administrative hurdles that had threatened to derail my aspirations.

This moment of triumph proved short-lived. Within a week, the university released the official results, which classified me in the third division with less than 50% marks. The discrepancy stemmed from an inexplicable administrative error: I had been marked "absent" in both English Literature papers—subjects in which I had not only appeared but expected to excel, given my longstanding interest in literature.

The weeks that followed involved exhausting journeys between Bikaner and Ajmer, pleading with university clerks to rectify what was clearly a clerical mistake. The provisional result they had provided earlier had indicated 50% overall marks, creating a contradictory paper trail that even the bureaucracy couldn't easily dismiss.

"How could I have been given a provisional result showing 50% if I was absent for two papers?" I argued repeatedly to increasingly uncomfortable administrators.

After numerous visits and appeals to increasingly senior officials, the truth emerged: the papers containing my English scores had been misplaced after being pulled from the regular batch to prepare my provisional result. Eventually, the clerks agreed to consult their copy of the previously prepared "confidential" provisional result and adjust my official record accordingly.

Armed with a revised marksheet and provisional degree certificate, I finally joined my MBA classes—two weeks late and with the peculiar distinction of having "barely passed" in subjects I had expected to excel in. The irony of achieving minimum passing marks in Economics and English Literature—disciplines I had genuinely enjoyed and performed well in—was overshadowed by relief at having overcome the administrative obstacle.

This experience reinforced a lesson that military life had already begun teaching me: systems, whether military or civilian, often operate with bureaucratic logic that bears little relationship to individual merit or circumstance. Success requires not just academic or professional competence but also persistence in navigating institutional barriers that seem designed to test resilience rather than ability.

Cultural Shift: The Making of an "Elite"

My delayed arrival at IMS Bikaner coincided with the peak of "introduction sessions" organised by senior students—a euphemistic term for the modified ragging that constituted an unofficial orientation to business school culture. These sessions, while avoiding physical violence, involved deliberate provocations designed to test junior students' composure under pressure—a crude simulation of the corporate environments we were preparing to enter.

"The trick," a sympathetic senior advised quietly, "is maintaining calm and poise through both civilised and occasionally uncivilised insults. Consider it preparation for dealing with unreasonable clients and temperamental bosses."

For someone raised in military environments, where discipline was enforced through structured hierarchies rather than psychological intimidation, these interactions initially seemed peculiar. However, my childhood exposure to military training had instilled resilience that made these challenges relatively manageable. Having witnessed the rigorous physical and mental conditioning that military cadets endured to maintain composure under genuine adversity, the theatrical provocations of business school hazing seemed almost quaint by comparison.

"Is this supposed to be difficult?" I asked a fellow junior after a particularly intense session. "Compared to what military cadets experience, this feels like a children's game."

More troubling than the hazing itself was the underlying ideology it seemed designed to instil—a deliberate cultivation of elitism that contradicted my egalitarian values. Senior students repeatedly emphasised that as future corporate executives, we occupied a privileged position in the social hierarchy, distinct from and superior to the "masses" and working classes.

This artificial stratification extended beyond the classroom to social interactions. While my friendship with the principal's son from Rampuria College remained acceptable within this new social order, my other friend—the "son-of-the-soil" Marwari classmate who had welcomed me into his family home—was now considered inappropriate company. The unspoken expectation that I should sever connections with friends deemed insufficiently "elite" struck me not merely as snobbish but as fundamentally contrary to the values of loyalty and camaraderie that military life had instilled.

"I'm not going to pretend I don't know him just because I'm doing an MBA now," I informed a senior who had commented disapprovingly on my continued association with my Rampuria friend. "Friendship isn't conditional on social status."

This resistance to artificial social boundaries would characterise my approach throughout business school and beyond—accepting the technical training while rejecting the implicit social conditioning that often accompanied it. The tension between professional advancement and personal values would remain a recurring theme throughout my career, requiring continuous negotiation between competing priorities.

The MBA programme itself represented a significant departure from undergraduate education, with smaller class sizes (thirty students compared to seventy-plus in college), more interactive teaching methods, and greater emphasis on practical applications. The curriculum balanced theoretical foundations with case studies and projects designed to simulate real-world business challenges, providing valuable preparation for professional environments.

My academic performance improved markedly in this setting, particularly in subjects related to economics and finance, where my genuine interest facilitated deeper engagement with the material. This improvement reflected not just greater application but also the alignment between the curriculum and my natural inclinations—a reminder that academic success often depends as much on finding the right educational environment as on individual ability.

Teaching Economics and New Business Competition

As the first semester progressed, I encountered an unexpected opportunity that would reveal a latent talent and potential career path. My Economics professor from Rampuria College, who also taught Managerial Economics in the MBA programme, asked me to conduct a class session on the concept of consumer surplus—a microeconomic principle describing the difference between what consumers are willing to pay for a product and what they actually pay.

"You seemed to grasp this concept particularly well," he explained when I expressed surprise at the request. "Sometimes students understand better when concepts are explained by peers who've recently mastered the material themselves."

Despite initial nervousness about addressing postgraduate students as an instructor rather than a classmate, I discovered a natural affinity for teaching. The session proceeded smoothly, with my explanation incorporating diagrammatic representations, mathematical expressions, and practical applications to market demand and pricing strategies. The positive response from both classmates and the professor suggested that I possessed communication skills that could translate complex concepts into accessible explanations—an ability that would prove valuable throughout my professional life.

"You have a gift for this," the professor commented afterwards. "Have you considered teaching as a career option?"

This experience revealed an aspect of my personality that military upbringing and academic training had cultivated: the ability to organise information logically, present it clearly, and respond effectively to questions—skills that military briefings and NCC presentations had developed long before I considered their professional applications. The satisfaction derived from successfully communicating complex ideas and witnessing others' understanding would remain a significant motivator throughout my career, even when my professional path led away from formal teaching roles.

The Economics professor further enhanced our learning through an innovative group competition that bridged theoretical knowledge with practical application. Each team was assigned to develop an economic case for establishing a new business, selecting from various small and medium-scale industries operating in and around Bikaner—ceramic production, traditional Bikaneri bhujia (spicy snack food), woollen textiles, leather goods, and dairy products.

Our group selected ceramic-tile manufacturing, with team members dividing responsibilities according to their strengths and interests. Having established credibility through my classroom teaching experience, I naturally assumed responsibility for the economic analysis—developing cost functions, determining optimal pricing and production volumes based on cost–revenue relationships, and calculating break-even points necessary for business viability. Other team members focused on technical specifications, operational requirements, and marketing strategies, creating a comprehensive business plan that integrated multiple perspectives.

This project provided valuable experience in collaborative problem-solving and practical application of theoretical concepts—skills directly relevant to real-world business environments. The process of researching actual market conditions, analysing industry-specific cost structures, and developing financially viable business models offered insights that purely theoretical exercises could never provide.

Our group's presentation earned top honours in the competition, with judges particularly commending the economic analysis that supported our business case. This success reinforced my growing confidence in applying economic principles to practical business challenges—a capability that would prove valuable throughout my subsequent career, even as specific applications evolved with changing professional contexts.

The project also demonstrated the value of integrating theoretical education with practical, real-world applications—an approach that senior students noted had not been included in previous curricula. This innovation reflected the evolving nature of management education in India during the early 1990s, as institutions increasingly recognised the importance of practical experience alongside theoretical foundations.

The Hanuman Group: Brotherhood of the Perpetually Single

Social dynamics within our MBA cohort quickly crystallised into distinct groups, with one particular formation earning the colourful designation "Hanuman Group"—a reference to the celibate monkey god that humorously characterised our collective status as perpetually single males. This group of eight students, myself included, developed a reputation for behaviour that simultaneously entertained and alarmed the broader college community.

The nickname carried multiple layers of meaning within the Indian cultural context. Lord Hanuman represents the eternal bachelor deity in Hindu mythology, embodying strength, loyalty, and celibacy. In student culture, however, "Hanuman Group" carried a different connotation—referring to males who remained single not by spiritual choice but through social rejection, particularly by female classmates who avoided their company for various reasons.

These reasons typically included excessive use of profanity, desperate behaviour around women that occasionally bordered on inappropriate, confrontational attitudes toward authority figures, and exaggerated displays of masculine bravado. While not every member exhibited all these characteristics, the group collectively embodied enough of them to earn its distinctive designation.

My own inclusion in this brotherhood represented a significant departure from my previous "good boy" persona. Having avoided profanity throughout school and undergraduate studies, I suddenly found myself adopting the colourful vocabulary that served as verbal currency within the group—expressions that members jokingly referred to as "helping verbs" that added emphasis to communication rather than conveying specific meaning.

Our academic behaviour further cemented the group's reputation. Three members consistently arrived late for classes, two regularly consumed Phensedyl (a mild narcotic cough syrup) during lectures under the pretence of treating throat infections, while others (myself included) developed such a thorough command of technical subjects like finance and economics that we occasionally challenged professors' explanations—behaviour that faculty understandably found disruptive regardless of its academic merit.

Despite these problematic behaviours, the Hanuman Group possessed redeeming qualities that earned grudging respect from peers and seniors alike. Our willingness to accept challenging assignments, ability to execute complex projects under tight deadlines, and genuine camaraderie created a functional team dynamic that produced impressive results when properly directed.

This capability became evident when we volunteered to organise the farewell party for graduating seniors—a task typically requiring months of planning that we compressed into a single week. The event included elaborate cultural performances, personalised recognition for each departing student, catered food service, and even unofficial post-ceremony celebrations involving alcoholic beverages (strictly prohibited on campus but traditionally included in such events through discreet arrangements).

The success of this hastily organised celebration demonstrated the group's capacity for effective collaboration when motivated by appropriate challenges. The seniors departed impressed by our organisational abilities, professors expressed surprised appreciation for our execution, and even the institute administration acknowledged the event's success despite their awareness of its unsanctioned elements.

Following the official celebration, our group conducted our own private gathering with leftover refreshments, creating improvised music and lyrics that, while unprintable in respectable publications, cemented our bonds through shared transgression and creativity. This after-party, extending into early morning hours, exemplified both the problematic and positive aspects of our collective identity—simultaneously reinforcing behavioural patterns that limited our social acceptance while strengthening internal cohesion that supported academic and organisational achievements.

The Hanuman Group represented my first experience with a self-selected social identity distinct from the institutional affiliations that had previously defined my social positioning. Unlike military community membership or school enrolment, which assigned social roles based on external factors, this association reflected personal choice and affinity—a significant step in developing independent social identity beyond institutional frameworks.

This experience provided valuable lessons about group dynamics that would prove relevant throughout my professional career. I observed how collective identity could simultaneously enhance performance through mutual support while enabling problematic behaviours through diffused responsibility. The group's ability to accomplish impressive results despite (or perhaps because of) its unconventional approaches demonstrated that effective teamwork doesn't always conform to organisational ideals of professional behaviour—an insight that would inform my later management of diverse teams with varying work styles and personal characteristics.

Industrial Tour, Lovestruck, and Disaster

December 1993 brought our junior MBA batch's industrial tour to Delhi—an educational excursion that would provide unexpected lessons in both professional and personal domains. The journey began with an overnight train ride through Rajasthan's winter landscape, our second-class sleeper coach filled with thirty enthusiastic students determined to extract maximum enjoyment from this rare excursion beyond Bikaner's familiar boundaries.

The overnight journey created a festive atmosphere as we sang and danced well into the night, temporarily setting aside academic pressures in favour of youthful camaraderie. When the train halted at Ratangarh junction near Churu—renowned as Rajasthan's coldest location, where winter temperatures regularly plunged below freezing—we disembarked briefly to sample the station's famous kulhad doodh (unskimmed milk served in earthen cups), its thick layer of cream providing welcome warmth against the biting cold.

"Look at these MBA students celebrating with milk!" commented an amused bystander, observing our enthusiastic consumption of this simple refreshment. "Acting like they're having a booze party in the middle of the night!"

The comment highlighted the innocent nature of our revelry compared to typical student excursions—a reflection of both our relatively sheltered backgrounds and the limited entertainment options available in small-town Rajasthan during the early 1990s.

Upon reaching Delhi, our educational programme included lectures at the Management Department of the Indian Institute of Technology (IIT Delhi), where one particular marketing professor made a lasting impression through his unconventional approach. Rather than delivering standard marketing theory to visiting students already studying the subject at their home institution, he chose to share personal insights about life beyond academic frameworks.

"All boys are broken hearts and all girls are cut noses," he declared with the confidence of someone sharing profound wisdom rather than questionable generalisations. His statement, translated from Hindi, suggested that most young men carried stories of failed (often unrequited) romantic attachments, while young women frequently complained of "Naak Kat Gayi" (literally "nose cut off")—an idiomatic expression for losing face or suffering embarrassment in social contexts.

This dubious psychological observation was followed by equally questionable practical advice: when attempting to initiate conversation with an unfamiliar woman at social gatherings, he recommended approaching someone standing alone and asking, "Why are you so sensitive?" This approach, he assured us with complete conviction, would invariably create a positive impression and potential romantic interest.

The professor's amateur psychology and dating advice, while entertaining, seemed harmless enough until I foolishly decided to test his theories. A female classmate had caught my attention through her soft-spoken demeanour and musical voice, qualities that appealed to my appreciation for gentleness and artistic sensibility. Our collaboration on the award-winning business case project had provided opportunities for interaction that reinforced my growing interest, though I remained unaware that she had already begun a relationship with another classmate.

My friend from S.D. College Ambala, who happened to be in Delhi during our visit, encouraged this romantic inclination when I confided my interest during an evening at his home. As we reminisced about our Ambala days over pizza and Thumbs Up cola, he suggested the traditional approach of offering flowers and a greeting card expressing my feelings—seemingly safer advice than the marketing professor's questionable tactics.

That evening, ZEE TV premiered Mahesh Bhatt's romantic musical Phir Teri Kahani Yaad Aayi, whose melancholic love songs—particularly "Baadalon Mein Chhup Rahaa Hai Chaand Kyun…"—provided a soundtrack to my imagined romantic future. The combination of emotional music, encouraging friendship, and youthful optimism created a potent mixture that overwhelmed my usually cautious nature.

Upon returning to Bikaner, I composed a New Year greeting card addressed to my classmate at the IMS Bikaner address. Rather than signing my name, I cryptically wrote "guess who?" and concluded with the marketing professor's recommended phrase: "Why are you so sensitive?" This anonymous approach, intended as intriguing rather than unsettling, represented my first significant miscalculation in what would become a cascade of romantic misjudgments.

The second critical error involved seeking advice from my Hanuman Group friends regarding the next steps after sending the anonymous card. Their guidance—observing her reaction to the message and approaching her when alone to reveal myself as the sender—failed to consider the fundamental inappropriateness of the situation or the potential for misinterpretation.

"Never listen to Hanumans in matters of the heart," I would later advise others, having learned this lesson through painful experience. "They'll ensure you fail so miserably that you'll wish for the earth to swallow you alive."

Following my friends' misguided counsel, I approached my classmate during lunch break after they had observed her reading the card with what they described as "bewilderment" (which I would later recognise as irritation). Gathering my courage, I asked whether she had received my card—the one signed "guess who?"

Her response was immediate and unequivocal: "I didn't expect that from you."

This statement, delivered with evident disappointment rather than the hoped-for interest, conveyed that she had held me in higher regard than my actions now warranted. Rather than recognising this clear rejection, I remained standing before her, prompting her direct question: "What do you want?"

In this crucial moment, my literary background and appreciation for poetry should have provided numerous eloquent expressions of romantic interest. Instead, influenced by the crude vocabulary that had become habitual within the Hanuman Group, I heard myself uttering words that horrified me even as they left my mouth: "I want an intimate relationship with you."

This catastrophically inappropriate declaration—combining the worst elements of clinical detachment and presumptuous familiarity—effectively terminated any potential for positive interaction. She walked away without further comment, leaving me standing in bewildered embarrassment as my so-called friends observed from a distance, their amusement at my humiliation evident in their expressions.

The consequences of this disastrous attempt at romantic expression extended throughout our remaining three semesters at IMS. We became effectively invisible to each other—passing in corridors without acknowledgement, participating in classes without interaction, and attending events without recognition. This mutual non-existence strategy preserved superficial civility while avoiding the awkwardness of addressing what had occurred.

The final ironic punctuation to this romantic disaster came during our farewell celebration, where I performed Shah Rukh Khan's song "Jaadu Teri Nazar…" from the film Darr—a movie featuring an obsessive stalker as protagonist. My off-key rendition, concluding with the ominous lyric "Chheen Lungaa Tujhey Iss Jahaan Sey…" (I'll snatch you away from this world), inadvertently reinforced the very impression I had hoped to overcome.

This experience, while personally mortifying, provided valuable lessons about communication, context, and consent that would inform my future interactions. I learned that romantic expressions require appropriate timing, mutual interest, and contextual awareness—considerations that neither marketing professors nor Hanuman Group members had incorporated into their misguided advice.

Predicting the Union Budget and Extempore Speech

My academic interests found constructive expression through opportunities that aligned with my genuine passions rather than misguided social experiments. Throughout my undergraduate studies, I had approached Economics not merely as an academic subject but as a practical framework for understanding national development—often imagining myself in the Finance Minister's position, weighing policy options that might stimulate India's economic potential.

This perspective found practical application when IMS authorities asked students to organise pre-budget and post-budget seminars coinciding with the Union Budget presentation in March 1994. Senior government officials from the state finance department were invited to participate, creating a professional forum for economic discussion that transcended typical classroom exercises.

As the unofficial "economist" of our batch, I naturally assumed responsibility for presenting recommendations regarding potential budget measures to stimulate economic growth. Drawing on my understanding of macroeconomic principles and India's specific developmental challenges, I outlined policy proposals that balanced fiscal responsibility with growth initiatives—an approach that impressed the government officials in attendance.

When the actual budget was announced the following day, I was astonished to discover that approximately 60% of my predictions aligned with measures implemented by Finance Minister Dr Manmohan Singh. This coincidence generated considerable satisfaction—not from any presumption that my ideas had influenced national policy but from the validation that my economic reasoning paralleled that of respected policymakers.

"Either great minds think alike," joked a classmate, "or you've tapped the Finance Ministry's phone lines."

This period represented a pivotal moment in India's economic history—the early years of liberalisation following the 1991 balance of payments crisis that had forced the mortgaging of national gold reserves. The Harshad Mehta securities scam remained fresh in public consciousness, while inflation and foreign exchange challenges continued to constrain economic potential. Against this backdrop, the government's reform agenda represented a dramatic departure from decades of centralised economic planning toward greater market orientation.

Our post-budget analysis session became a celebration of both our analytical capabilities and the government's continued commitment to economic reforms. As students preparing to enter the business world, we recognised that these policy changes would shape the professional landscape we would soon navigate—creating both opportunities and challenges that previous generations of Indian managers had not encountered.

This experience reinforced my interest in economic policy as a framework for national development—a perspective that would influence my professional choices throughout subsequent decades. The satisfaction derived from accurately analysing complex economic factors and predicting their policy implications suggested potential career paths that combined analytical capabilities with practical impact on development outcomes.

My public speaking abilities found further expression through extempore speech competitions that tested improvisational capabilities alongside content knowledge. One particularly memorable contest occurred at Maharani College, Bikaner's prestigious women's institution that remained largely inaccessible to male students from Rampuria College but welcomed participants from the "elite" IMS for competitive events.

The competition format was particularly challenging: participants selected topics by random draw and immediately began speaking without preparation time. When my turn came, I approached the stage with trepidation, opened my assigned topic, and discovered the prompt: "Qualities I would like in my would-be spouse."

The irony of addressing this topic—standing before an audience of hundreds of young women shortly after my disastrous romantic overture—was not lost on me. Rather than attempting humour or personal anecdotes that might have further damaged my already compromised romantic credibility, I chose a philosophical approach that elevated the discussion beyond individual preferences.

My impromptu speech explored the complementary nature of masculine and feminine energies, referencing the concept of "Ardhanarishvara" (the composite androgynous form of Shiva and Parvati) to illustrate marriage as a divine fusion creating complete personality through the balanced integration of complementary characteristics. This abstract approach, while perhaps disappointing audience members expecting a practical discussion of relationship dynamics, impressed judges sufficiently to earn third prize in the competition.

A similar competition during IMS Bikaner's "Management Week" presented an even greater improvisational challenge when my randomly assigned topic proved to be "If I were a frog." The absurdity of this prompt momentarily paralysed my thinking until I noticed my unrequited romantic interest in the audience—recalling that her undergraduate studies in zoology had included dissecting live frogs.

This association triggered an unexpected emotional response that transformed potential embarrassment into compelling performance. I channelled the fear and pain that laboratory frogs might experience into a first-person narrative, later transitioning to childhood memories of catching tadpoles in monsoon puddles—creating unexpected emotional resonance from a seemingly ridiculous prompt.

The audience's enthusiastic response—laughing at humorous moments while connecting with underlying emotional content—earned first prize in this competition. This success demonstrated that effective communication often emerges from authentic emotional connection rather than technical perfection—a principle that would inform my approach to professional communication throughout my subsequent career.

These experiences collectively reinforced my growing recognition that communication abilities represented a significant professional asset regardless of specific career path. Whether analysing economic policies, addressing philosophical concepts, or transforming absurd prompts into engaging narratives, the capacity to organise thoughts coherently and present them effectively would prove valuable across diverse professional contexts.

Summer Training and the Struggle in Delhi

The transition from academic theory to professional practice arrived with the summer internship between the second and third semesters—an experience that provided a harsh introduction to corporate realities far removed from classroom idealisations. Another member of the Hanuman Group and I secured two-month unpaid internships at Pantaloon Fashions in Delhi, expecting valuable exposure to retail marketing strategies and brand management practices.

The reality proved dramatically different from these expectations. Rather than engaging with strategic marketing concepts, we discovered that interns occupied the lowest rung of the corporate hierarchy—"expendables" assigned tasks that regular employees preferred to avoid. Our project officially involved developing brand-positioning maps for Bare jeans and Knighthood shirts relative to competitors. Still, daily responsibilities primarily consisted of visiting retail showrooms throughout Delhi, carrying product samples, and attempting to convince store owners to stock Pantaloon merchandise.

This glorified sales role required traversing Delhi's sprawling geography during peak summer heat and early monsoon humidity—conditions made more challenging by our limited financial resources. Coming from modest backgrounds with fathers serving as technical ground crew in the Air Force, we could afford only basic accommodation in Sagarpur—an area I would later recognise as one of Delhi's numerous slum settlements during professional work on urban health issues.

Our daily routine involved crowded Delhi Transport Corporation bus journeys across the city, with no budget for breakfast, lunch limited to questionably hygienic fruit salads from street vendors, and dinner typically consisting of two boiled eggs. This austere existence during Delhi's most punishing weather season—temperatures regularly exceeding 40°C with humidity levels approaching 90% during early monsoon—created physical challenges that frequently resulted in illness.

"This is what they mean by 'paying your dues' in the corporate world," my internship partner observed grimly as we hung from overhead rails in an overcrowded bus, sweat-soaked and exhausted after another day of rejections from high-end retailers who showed little interest in our product samples.

These experiences provided a visceral understanding of urban poverty that theoretical discussions could never convey. Travelling through Delhi in a physically depleted state—dizzy from heat, weakened by inadequate nutrition, and constantly balancing on the edge of collapse—created unexpected empathy with the city's manual labourers whose daily existence involved similar challenges: rickshaw pullers straining against impossible loads in suffocating heat; construction workers carrying head-loads of bricks up precarious scaffolding; street vendors standing for endless hours in direct sunlight.

This perspective would later inform my professional engagement with urban poverty issues, providing an experiential foundation that academic research alone could not supply. When participating in policy discussions about urban development and poverty reduction in later years, I would recall the physical sensation of near-collapse while hanging from a bus rail—remembering that theoretical solutions meant little without understanding the embodied reality of those experiencing poverty firsthand.

Midway through this challenging internship, my father's transfer to Bagdogra air base in eastern India created additional emotional complexity. During his brief layover in Delhi while travelling from Bikaner to his new posting, he observed my deteriorated physical condition with evident concern. Despite my technical ineligibility for military medical services as a dependent over eighteen years old, he arranged an examination at the Medical Inspection (MI) room at Sainik Aaraamghar (soldiers' rest house) near Old Delhi railway station, listing my age as eighteen to secure treatment.

This small deception highlighted the approaching severance of my connection to military support systems that had provided security throughout childhood and adolescence. The realisation that I now existed primarily as a civilian—one face among millions navigating urban challenges without institutional protection—reinforced the significance of this transitional period between military childhood and civilian adulthood.

Despite these challenges, we completed our assigned project successfully, developing comprehensive brand-positioning maps that impressed the Zonal Manager sufficiently to earn token compensation of one thousand rupees each—our first corporate income. This modest sum represented a significant achievement given our unpaid internship status, and I immediately invested in professional attire: a formal two-piece suit, branded jeans, and a casual shirt that would support the transition from student to professional appearance.

The internship's difficulties provided a valuable perspective on corporate realities that classroom discussions had sanitised or idealised. I learned that organisational hierarchies often functioned differently from how organisational charts suggested, that theoretical knowledge required practical application to generate value, and that physical resilience sometimes proved as important as intellectual capability in professional environments. These insights, while painfully acquired, would inform my approach to subsequent career challenges and management responsibilities.

Unfair Means Case

The completion of summer training should have represented a straightforward transition to final-year studies, but administrative complications once again threatened my academic progress. Although my internship partner and I had both completed projects at Pantaloon Fashions, Delhi, we had focused on different product lines—I analysed Knighthood shirts while he examined Bare jeans—resulting in distinct reports despite the shared organisational context.

The preparation of these reports involved accessing computer facilities at private training institutes during evening hours when regular classes had concluded. This arrangement reflected the limited access to technology available to students in mid-1990s India, when personal computers were luxury items rather than standard educational tools. After completing our separate documents using different software applications—text in WordStar, tables in Lotus 1-2-3, and graphs in Harvard Graphics—we arranged for printing on dot-matrix printers, which were the standard technology of the era.

While my partner's report printed successfully, mechanical failure interrupted the production of my document halfway through the process. The midnight hour and the next morning's submission deadline created a crisis situation with limited options for resolution. Attempting to resolve the printing problem somehow corrupted my document files, eliminating the possibility of reprinting, even if the mechanical issues could be addressed.

"There's no time to recreate everything," my partner observed pragmatically. "Since we both did internships at the same company, why not submit identical reports? Just photocopy mine and submit it with your name."

This suggestion, born of desperation rather than dishonest intent, seemed reasonable given our shared internship context and the technical failure that had destroyed my original work.

Without fully considering potential consequences, I agreed to this expedient solution—a decision that would return with significant repercussions just before final examinations.

The institution head summoned both of us to his office with grave news: submitting identical reports constituted a clear case of cheating under university regulations. This "Unfair Means Case" (UMC) could result in termination of our MBA degrees and rustication from the university—consequences dramatically disproportionate to our pragmatic but ill-considered solution to a technical problem.

"I'm willing to give you one opportunity to salvage your futures," he offered, his expression conveying both disappointment and reluctant compassion. "Submit different summer training reports within two weeks of completing your MBA final examinations, and I'll consider the matter resolved."

This unexpected requirement created additional pressure during an already stressful examination period, forcing me to identify an alternative project that could be quickly completed and documented. The physical and mental challenges experienced during the original internship—which had genuinely provided valuable learning despite our documentation problems—were effectively erased from the institutional record, replaced by a hastily assembled report on incomplete projects at Rajasthan Finance Corporation's Bikaner district office.

This experience highlighted the sometimes arbitrary nature of academic integrity standards that focused on documentation procedures rather than learning outcomes. While understanding the importance of independent work and proper attribution in academic contexts, the disproportionate consequences threatened for what was essentially a pragmatic response to technical failure rather than intentional plagiarism seemed to prioritise procedural compliance over genuine learning.

Challenging Authority: The Price of Academic Defiance

The Hanuman Group's penchant for challenging authority extended beyond social transgressions into academic domains, particularly when it came to technical subjects like finance and economics. This confrontational approach—what we called taking panga with authorities—manifested in various forms, from questioning established procedures to directly challenging professors' expertise. While this behaviour reflected genuine intellectual curiosity and commitment to understanding, it often created friction with faculty members unaccustomed to having their knowledge contested by students.

My own participation in this pattern of academic defiance would eventually extract a significant price. As we progressed to specialisation subjects in the second year of the MBA programme, I naturally gravitated toward Finance, with a particular interest in investment and portfolio management. The analytical frameworks and quantitative methodologies aligned perfectly with my intellectual inclinations, providing structured approaches to evaluating complex economic systems.

When selecting my dissertation topic, I developed a specific interest in equity research methodologies—particularly the contrast between technical analysis (focused on price movements and trading patterns) and fundamental analysis (examining underlying business value and economic factors). While technical analysis dominated market practice due to its utility for short-term trading, I found myself drawn to fundamental analysis as a framework for identifying long-term growth opportunities that aligned with broader economic developments.

"I'd like to focus my dissertation on using fundamental analysis to identify stocks with strong long-term growth potential," I informed my professor during our initial consultation regarding dissertation topics.

His response was immediately discouraging. "That would require projecting inflation over your investment horizon—a complex macroeconomic modelling exercise that's beyond the scope of an MBA dissertation. I won't be able to provide much guidance if you pursue that direction."

This discouragement, rather than deterring my interest, transformed the project into a personal challenge—an opportunity to demonstrate capabilities beyond expected academic parameters. The professor's scepticism became motivation to prove that sophisticated economic analysis remained accessible even without specialised computational resources or advanced econometric training.

Drawing on government Five-Year Plan documents and industry projections published in Capital Market magazine, I constructed macroeconomic models that projected inflation rates over a five-year investment horizon. This analysis provided the foundation for identifying growth sectors likely to outperform during this period, ultimately yielding the selection of specific securities projected to deliver annualised returns exceeding 20%.

The methodology integrated multiple analytical layers—macroeconomic forecasting, sector-specific growth projections, and company-level fundamental analysis—creating a comprehensive investment framework that exceeded typical MBA dissertation scope. When later comparing my inflation projections with those produced by the National Council for Applied Economic Research (NCAER) using sophisticated computational models, I discovered my estimates deviated by merely 0.06 percentage points—validation of both the methodology and execution that provided immense satisfaction.

The dissertation defence before external examiners proved triumphant, with evaluators expressing particular appreciation for the ambitious scope and methodological rigour. Their positive response suggested that my academic defiance had been justified—that pushing beyond conventional expectations had produced genuinely valuable work deserving recognition.

This triumph proved short-lived, however, when final results were announced. Despite successful defence and positive examiner feedback, my result was withheld with the notation that I had been marked "absent" for the dissertation submission—effectively failing this crucial component despite having completed and defended it successfully.

The cruel irony of this situation—being marked absent for work I had not only submitted but successfully defended—echoed my earlier experience with English Literature papers during undergraduate studies. Once again, administrative systems had created an artificial barrier to academic progress through inexplicable procedural failure.

"How could I have been given scores in the viva examination if my dissertation was never submitted?" I asked repeatedly during appeals to university authorities. "The external examiner's comments clearly reference specific aspects of my written work."

Despite having duplicate copies of the dissertation available, the institute head initially refused to accept "late submission," maintaining that original documentation deadlines were absolute regardless of circumstances. This rigid procedural stance—prioritising administrative formalities over demonstrated academic achievement—exemplified the bureaucratic mindset that often impedes genuine educational advancement in institutional settings.

The resolution required months of persistent appeals, eventually resulting in the university's agreement to consider my duplicate dissertation copy. However, the administrative delay meant that official degree confirmation came two years after completing coursework—creating professional complications as I entered the workforce with only provisional certification of my qualifications.

This pattern would extend remarkably far into my future, with the provisional certificate serving as my credential for nearly three decades of professional life. Even when completing doctoral studies in Business Finance at a Swiss business school in 2025, my application relied on the provisional MBA certificate rather than original degree documentation. The original degree certificate finally reached my hands only in 2023—twenty-eight years after completing the programme—providing belated official recognition of qualifications that had shaped my entire professional trajectory.

This experience reinforced important lessons about institutional systems and personal resilience. While academic defiance—challenging conventional limitations and pursuing ambitious intellectual goals—can produce valuable results that exceed standard expectations, it often triggers institutional resistance that extracts significant personal cost. The systems designed to certify achievement frequently become obstacles to genuine innovation, requiring persistent advocacy to overcome procedural barriers that have little relationship to actual learning or capability.

Yet despite these frustrations, the experience confirmed that pursuing intellectual challenges aligned with genuine interests ultimately proves more valuable than conforming to limited expectations. The analytical capabilities developed through this ambitious project would serve me throughout subsequent professional endeavours, providing methodological foundations that transcended specific academic credentials. The dissertation experience demonstrated that meaningful learning often occurs precisely when pushing beyond comfortable boundaries—a principle that would guide my approach to professional development throughout subsequent decades.

The Rat Temple Adventure: Tempting Fate in the Desert Heat

As our MBA programme approached conclusion in May 1995, the Hanuman Group determined to commemorate our academic journey with one final adventure before dispersing toward our respective professional futures. We selected Deshnok—a small settlement thirty kilometres from Bikaner along the route toward Nagaur, Merta, and Ajmer—as our destination, drawn by its famous temple dedicated to Karni Mata, the patron deity of Bikaner's royal family.

According to local tradition, Karni Mata—a female mystic believed to embody divine energy—had blessed Rao Bikaji and instructed him to establish his capital at Bikaner in 1488 CE. This historical connection made the temple significant to local cultural identity, with Karni Mata functioning as the presiding spiritual guardian of the region. As we prepared to leave Bikaner for our professional journeys, seeking her blessing seemed an appropriate symbolic closure to our time in the desert city.

The temple's international reputation, however, stemmed from its unusual residents rather than its historical significance. Known colloquially as "Chuhaa Mandir" (Rat Temple), the site housed thousands of rats considered sacred disciples of the goddess. These rodents received offerings of milk, grains, and sweets from both priests and visitors, growing fat and numerous under this divine protection. Local belief held that accidentally killing one of these sacred rats required atonement through offering gold equal to the deceased rodent's weight—a potentially expensive mistake for careless visitors. Conversely, glimpsing a rare white rat within the temple promised exceptional good fortune—a prospect that particularly appealed to young graduates facing uncertain professional futures.

Planning our expedition required practical considerations alongside spiritual aspirations. The extreme desert climate meant temperatures regularly exceeded 50 degrees Celsius during midday and afternoon hours, making early-morning departure essential for comfortable travel. We arranged to meet at dawn, with transportation provided by my Hero Puch moped and a friend's Bajaj scooter—modest vehicles for desert travel, but the only options available within our limited student budgets.

My journey began inauspiciously when, riding from my family's home in Lalgarh toward my friends' accommodation near IMS in pre-dawn darkness, I encountered stray dogs engaged in territorial combat. Two fighting canines collided with my front tyre while I travelled at approximately 45 kilometres per hour, sending me crashing to the pavement. I instinctively protected my head during the fall, but landed heavily on my left elbow, the impact tearing away skin and tissue to expose the underlying bone.

Strangely, the injury produced minimal immediate pain—likely due to shock and adrenaline—allowing me to assess the damage to both body and vehicle with surprising detachment. My glasses and the moped's headlight had shattered, but the vehicle remained operational despite cosmetic damage. Determining that both injury and mechanical issues were manageable, I continued toward my friends' accommodation, blood flowing freely from my wounded elbow as I navigated the dark streets.

Arriving at their residence, I encountered unexpected obstacles to our carefully planned early departure. Despite repeated bell-ringing and door-knocking, no response came from within. After fifteen increasingly desperate minutes—time that seemed interminable as blood dried on my arm and pain gradually emerged through receding shock—one friend finally opened the door, revealing the cause of their unresponsiveness.

The scene inside resembled the aftermath of a minor natural disaster: bodies sprawled across furniture and floor in various states of undress, empty liquor bottles scattered among half-eaten food, bedding and personal items strewn haphazardly throughout the space. My friends had apparently decided to commemorate our final night in Bikaner with an impromptu celebration, each consuming an entire bottle of inexpensive whisky before collapsing into alcohol-induced unconsciousness.

"What happened to you?" my barely conscious friend asked, noticing my bloodied condition with delayed comprehension.

"Dog fight," I replied tersely, anger at their condition temporarily overshadowing concern about my injury. "We were supposed to leave at dawn, remember?"

The transition from unconsciousness to travel-readiness required nearly four hours, during which my dried blood formed a makeshift seal over the exposed bone while my friends gradually processed both their hangovers and the seriousness of my injury. By the time our expedition finally departed, the desert sun had climbed high overhead, pushing temperatures beyond 50 degrees Celsius—precisely the punishing conditions we had hoped to avoid through early departure.

Our small convoy—my damaged moped carrying myself and one friend, while the Bajaj scooter transported three others—had travelled barely ten kilometres to Palana when the extreme heat caused my moped's piston to seize. This mechanical failure prompted predictable mockery from the scooter's owner, who proudly contrasted his vehicle's supposed reliability with my moped's limitations.

"This is why they call it 'Raja'," he boasted, patting his scooter's handlebars affectionately. "A king never abandons his subjects in difficult conditions!"

This premature celebration of mechanical superiority received cosmic rebuke just kilometres later when the scooter's tyre succumbed to heat-softened asphalt, developing a leak that required roadside repair. We replaced the damaged tyre with the spare and continued toward our destination, finally reaching Deshnok during peak afternoon heat.

The temple complex shimmered in the merciless sunlight, every surface reflecting heat that seemed to penetrate directly into our bodies despite minimal physical exertion. With no food available nearby and water supplies limited, we proceeded directly to the main shrine for darshan (divine viewing) of the deity, navigating carefully among the numerous rats that scurried across floors and surfaces throughout the temple.

Having received the goddess's blessing, we turned our attention toward the legendary white rat that supposedly conferred exceptional good fortune upon those fortunate enough to glimpse it. After considerable searching among the temple's many chambers and alcoves, one friend spotted a white tail disappearing into a small hole in the wall—a partial sighting that seemed insufficient for proper blessing.

"We can't leave with half-luck," declared the most impulsive member of our group, reaching decisively into the hole and grasping the retreating tail. With a single determined pull, he extracted the protesting white rodent, holding it aloft like a trophy while it squirmed indignantly in his grip.

"We're not waiting for luck to find us," he announced to startled temple visitors nearby. "We're taking our destiny into our own hands!"

This literal interpretation of a metaphorical concept—physically seizing good fortune rather than waiting for its appearance—exemplified the Hanuman Group's characteristic approach to life challenges. Whether through academic defiance, social transgression, or this sacrilegious manhandling of a sacred temple resident, we consistently rejected passive acceptance of established limitations in favour of direct intervention—sometimes with questionable judgement but always with complete commitment.

After releasing the understandably agitated rat and repairing the scooter's punctured tyre, we began our return journey with optimism that proved short-lived. Within five kilometres, the recently repaired tyre failed again, requiring another replacement with our dwindling supply of functional equipment. Ten kilometres further, another tyre failure left us without a spare—stranded in a barren desert landscape with no visible human presence, surrounded only by sand dunes and thorny vegetation under the punishing afternoon sun.

The temperature had climbed beyond 52 degrees Celsius, transforming the landscape into a shimmering hellscape where sand burned through shoe soles and metal surfaces became untouchable without protective cloth. We sought shelter beside a sand dune, huddling beneath a thorny bush while one friend—an engineering student with creative but questionable scientific understanding—attempted to improve our situation by rapidly moving a branch overhead.

"If I move the shadow quickly enough," he explained with complete seriousness, "it covers more area and keeps us all cooler."

This dubious physics demonstration—suggesting that rapidly moving a single shadow could somehow multiply its cooling effect—exemplified the delirious thinking that extreme heat can induce. Our collective response—contemplating whether to bury both him and his beloved scooter in the sand or simply abandon them to the elements—reflected similar heat-affected judgment, fortunately interrupted by the appearance of a truck on the distant road.

One friend flagged down the passing vehicle, securing transportation to Palana, where tyre repairs could be completed. The remaining hours of daylight disappeared during this process, meaning our return journey to Bikaner occurred during sunset and early evening—finally delivering us to my family home as darkness fell, nearly fifteen hours after our intended departure time.

My mother's reaction upon seeing my condition—dried blood caking my arm, exposed bone visible through damaged tissue, clothing and skin covered with desert dust—combined horror at my injury with disbelief at our collective recklessness. The family's railway doctor friend dressed my wound that evening, removing debris and applying proper antiseptic treatment that finally triggered the full pain response that shock and adrenaline had previously suppressed.

"This will leave a significant scar," he observed while wrapping bandages around my elbow. "A permanent reminder of today's adventure."

His prediction proved accurate—the scar remains visible decades later, a physical testament to youthful misadventure and the desert's unforgiving nature. This permanent marking seems an appropriate commemoration of the Hanuman Group's final expedition—a visible reminder that our collective identity, while sometimes enabling reckless behaviour, also fostered resilience and determination that transformed potential disasters into memorable adventures.

The Deshnok journey encapsulated essential qualities that defined our MBA experience: ambitious planning undermined by practical complications; determination to continue despite setbacks; willingness to improvise solutions with limited resources; and ultimately achieving objectives through persistence rather than perfect execution. These same qualities would serve us in professional environments where theoretical knowledge required adaptation to practical constraints, and where success often depended more on resilience than initial preparation.

Equity Research and Professional Beginnings

The transition from academic to professional life presented unexpected challenges as I completed my MBA programme in 1995. Having specialised in finance with a particular focus on equity research and investment analysis, I naturally sought positions with investment management firms and equity research departments where my analytical capabilities and macroeconomic understanding could find practical application.

The timing proved unfortunate, however, as India's financial sector continued recovering from the Harshad Mehta securities scam that had shaken market confidence and regulatory structures. Many investment firms had reduced operations or closed entirely, while those maintaining active research departments typically recruited exclusively from elite institutions like the Indian Institutes of Management (IIMs), considering graduates from regional programmes like IMS Bikaner insufficiently prestigious regardless of individual capability.

This situation created a professional dilemma—my technical skills and genuine interest aligned with financial analysis roles that remained largely inaccessible due to institutional pedigree rather than actual qualifications. The contradiction between meritocratic ideals emphasised during academic training and credential-based filtering that dominated actual hiring practices provided an early lesson in how professional advancement often depends on factors beyond individual performance or capability.

As weeks passed without promising opportunities in preferred fields, financial pressures mounted, and practical considerations began to outweigh ideal career trajectories. In this context, an unexpected opportunity arrived when a former senior from IMS Bikaner—then serving as Bikaner Division Manager for Times of India Group publications—visited my home with a potential employment proposition.

"I'm planning to start my own business and leave Times of India," he explained, "and need someone to replace my position here. Would you be interested in a media role focused on advertising and space marketing?"

The position represented a significant departure from my intended career path, involving sales-oriented responsibilities rather than financial analysis and focusing on media products rather than investment instruments. Yet practical considerations—steady income, established organisation, immediate availability—outweighed idealistic preferences given limited alternatives.

"Beggars can't be choosers," I reminded myself while considering the offer. "And perhaps marketing experience will prove valuable even if I eventually transition back toward finance."

Following a brief interview process that seemed largely formal, given my seniors' recommendation, I received an appointment letter as "Executive" with Times of India Group's Bikaner Division—marking the official commencement of my professional career. While the position didn't align with my academic specialisation or personal interests, it provided a stable foundation from which to begin professional development while continuing to explore opportunities more closely aligned with my financial analysis aspirations.

This compromise between ideal and practical considerations reflected a broader pattern that would characterise many subsequent career decisions—balancing personal interests against market realities, theoretical preferences against practical opportunities. The ability to adapt professional identity while maintaining core values and long-term objectives would prove essential throughout career transitions that followed, allowing flexibility without surrendering fundamental aspirations.

As I contemplated this first professional role while watching sunset illuminate Bikaner's desert landscape with characteristic golden light, complex emotions accompanied this transition moment. Excitement about beginning independent professional life mingled with apprehension about the corporate environment, so different from the military contexts that had shaped my childhood and adolescence. The impending separation from the Air Force community—which had provided both physical security and identity foundation throughout my formative years—created particular anxiety about navigating civilian professional culture without institutional support structures that had previously defined my social positioning.

"How will I reconcile my corporate professional identity with the military values and revolutionary ideals that shaped my worldview?" I wondered, watching darkness gradually claim the desert horizon. "Can I maintain commitment to justice and an equitable society while functioning within corporate structures designed primarily for profit generation?"

These questions reflected fundamental identity concerns rather than merely professional considerations—uncertainty about whether civilian corporate environments would accommodate the complex value system developed through military upbringing, political awakening during anti-Mandal protests, and intellectual exploration through literature and economics. The nomadic military childhood had instilled adaptability to changing physical environments but provided limited preparation for navigating value conflicts that might emerge when military-derived ethical frameworks encountered corporate priorities.

Yet alongside these concerns emerged recognition that military experience had provided valuable preparation for professional challenges in ways I hadn't fully appreciated. The lessons learned through constant relocation—adaptability to new circumstances, resilience through disruption, capacity to establish connections across diverse communities—represented transferable skills highly relevant to corporate environments experiencing rapid change during India's economic liberalisation.

Similarly, the self-discipline, organisational skills, and hierarchical awareness developed through proximity to military structures would prove valuable in corporate settings where similar qualities facilitated effective performance despite different specific applications. Even the political awareness developed during undergraduate years provided a useful perspective on organisational dynamics and power relationships that would influence professional advancement opportunities.

This recognition suggested the possibility that the apparent contradiction between military background and corporate future might actually represent complementary preparation—that values and capabilities developed through military childhood could find meaningful expression within civilian professional contexts, perhaps even offering a distinctive perspective that colleagues with more conventional backgrounds might lack.

As darkness completed its claim over the desert landscape, transforming golden sunset into a star-filled night sky, this reflection produced a tentative resolution to the identity questions that had accompanied my professional transition. Rather than abandoning military-derived values to accommodate corporate expectations, I would attempt integration—bringing military discipline, commitment to collective welfare, and strategic thinking into corporate contexts while adapting specific applications to new environmental requirements.

This integrative approach—maintaining core values while adapting their expression to changing contexts—would guide subsequent professional development through various roles and organisations. The capacity to function effectively within corporate structures without surrendering fundamental principles would prove essential to maintaining personal integrity while navigating professional advancement opportunities that inevitably involve compromise between ideal and practical considerations.

The desert chapter of my life was concluding, but its lessons would continue influencing my development through subsequent phases. Bikaner's harsh environment had taught resilience through adversity, appreciation for resources often taken for granted in more hospitable settings, and recognition that beauty exists even in seemingly barren landscapes for those willing to perceive it. These perspectives would inform my approach to professional challenges, interpersonal relationships, and personal development throughout adult life—desert wisdom applied to diverse circumstances far beyond Rajasthan's sand dunes.

Reflections on the Desert Years

Looking back on my time in Bikaner—from undergraduate studies at Rampuria College through the MBA programme at IMS and into my first professional position—several themes emerge that would shape my subsequent development. This desert interlude between military childhood and corporate adulthood functioned as a crucial transition space where identity components from different life phases could be integrated into a coherent adult personality capable of navigating complex professional and personal landscapes.

The academic journey through Bikaner's educational institutions provided important lessons about both formal knowledge acquisition and institutional navigation. The contrast between undergraduate and postgraduate experiences demonstrated how educational effectiveness depends not merely on institutional prestige but on alignment between teaching approaches and individual learning styles. While Rampuria College's traditional pedagogical methods had created friction with my more analytical and discussion-oriented preferences, IMS Bikaner's interactive approach and practical applications created a more productive learning environment despite both institutions occupying similar regional status within the Indian educational hierarchy.

The repeated administrative obstacles encountered during both undergraduate and postgraduate studies—from missing English Literature papers to a disappeared dissertation—provided valuable lessons about institutional systems and personal advocacy. These experiences demonstrated that organisational processes often operate according to internal logics disconnected from their ostensible purposes, requiring persistent intervention to achieve appropriate outcomes when standard procedures fail.

The skills developed through these administrative battles—documenting communications, identifying procedural contradictions, escalating concerns through appropriate channels, maintaining respectful persistence despite frustration—would prove valuable throughout subsequent professional life when navigating bureaucratic systems in various organisational contexts. The recognition that systems designed to facilitate achievement often become obstacles requiring navigation rather than mere compliance would inform my approach to organisational processes throughout career development.

Social experiences during this period—particularly the Hanuman Group dynamics and the failed romantic overture—provided important lessons about group identity, peer influence, and interpersonal communication. The contrast between my previous "good boy" persona and the more transgressive behaviours adopted within the Hanuman Group context demonstrated how social environment shapes individual behaviour, sometimes enabling actions inconsistent with core values when group identity becomes the primary reference point.

The romantic disaster resulting from misguided marketing professor advice and Hanuman Group encouragement provided painful but valuable lessons about communication context, consent, and appropriate expression of interest. This experience demonstrated the importance of authentic communication aligned with personal values rather than borrowed phrases or strategies incongruent with genuine character—a principle that would inform subsequent professional and personal interactions where authenticity consistently proved more effective than strategic calculation.

Professional preparation through the summer internship and initial job placement illustrated the significant gap between academic theory and practical application. The contrast between classroom discussions of strategic marketing concepts and the actual experience of carrying product samples through Delhi's sweltering streets demonstrated how organisational realities often differ dramatically from theoretical frameworks—

knowledge that would prove valuable when later developing training programmes that integrated practical applications with conceptual foundations.

The physical challenges encountered during the summer internship—heat exhaustion, inadequate nutrition, crowded transportation—created unexpected empathy with the urban working poor that theoretical discussions of poverty could never have generated. This embodied understanding of economic hardship would later inform my approach to development economics and poverty reduction initiatives, ensuring that technical solutions remained grounded in appreciation for lived experiences rather than abstract statistical representations.

Perhaps most significantly, this period facilitated the integration of seemingly contradictory identity components developed during different life phases. The military values instilled during childhood—discipline, service orientation, strategic thinking—found expression through academic achievements and group leadership despite the civilian educational context. The political awareness and social justice concerns developed during undergraduate years remained relevant despite professional preparation for corporate environments, which are often perceived as prioritising profit over equity considerations.

As I prepared to leave Bikaner for broader professional horizons, these desert years had transformed me from a military child into an independent adult with a distinctive perspective shaped by an unusual combination of influences—military discipline and academic analysis, traditional values and progressive aspirations, practical resilience and theoretical sophistication. This integrated identity would provide the foundation for navigating subsequent professional challenges while maintaining a connection to formative experiences that had shaped fundamental character.

As my time in Bikaner concluded with my first professional appointment, I couldn't have anticipated how profoundly these desert years would influence my subsequent life trajectory. The lessons learned through academic struggles, social experiments, and environmental challenges would provide reference points for navigating professional and personal decisions decades later—desert wisdom applied to circumstances far removed from Rajasthan's sand dunes.

The most enduring lesson emerged from the desert's fundamental duality—its capacity to appear simultaneously harsh and beautiful, threatening and nurturing, depending on perspective and preparation. This paradoxical quality taught an essential truth about challenging circumstances: that difficulty and opportunity often coexist within the same situations, with perception determining which becomes the dominant experience.

When facing professional setbacks in later years—projects that failed despite careful planning, promotions that went to less-qualified candidates, organisations that failed to recognise valuable contributions—I would recall desert journeys in which mechanical failures and physical injuries transformed routine excursions into memorable adventures. This perspective allowed recognition that apparent disasters often contain hidden opportunities when approached with resilience and creativity rather than despair.

Similarly, the desert's dramatic temperature fluctuations—blistering days followed by freezing nights—provided a metaphor for life's inevitable cycles of fortune and challenge. This pattern taught patience during difficult periods, knowing that conditions inevitably change for those prepared to endure temporary discomfort while maintaining focus on longer horizons. When professional environments later turned hostile or personal circumstances created temporary hardship, this desert wisdom provided reassurance that no condition, however extreme, remains permanent for those with the patience to await changing seasons.

Perhaps most importantly, the desert demonstrated that environments initially perceived as resource-poor often harbour unexpected abundance for those who learn to perceive appropriately. Just as desert dwellers recognise water sources, edible plants, and navigation markers invisible to untrained observers, I learned to identify opportunities and resources in professional contexts where others perceived only limitations. This capacity to recognise abundance within apparent scarcity would repeatedly create advantages throughout career development, allowing identification of unconventional paths forward when conventional routes appeared blocked.

The Bikaner years—spanning undergraduate studies, the MBA programme, and the first professional position—served as a crucial developmental phase in which military childhood experiences could be integrated with emerging adult identity. The desert provided an appropriate transitional space for this integration process—challenging enough to test the resilience developed through military upbringing, while offering opportunities to apply it toward academic and professional advancement rather than mere survival.

This integration process laid the foundation for a subsequent professional identity that maintained a connection to military values while functioning effectively in civilian contexts—discipline without rigidity, service orientation without institutional dependency, and strategic thinking without tactical limitations. The capacity to draw upon military-derived capabilities while adapting their application to corporate requirements would provide a distinctive perspective throughout professional development, allowing contributions that colleagues with more conventional backgrounds often couldn't envision.

As I departed Bikaner to begin a professional journey that would eventually span multiple organisations, sectors, and geographical regions, the desert had completed its transformative work—converting a military child into an independent professional with distinctive capabilities and perspectives. The harsh landscape that had initially appeared a temporary necessity had become an essential catalyst for personal development, providing exactly the challenging conditions required for identity integration and capability refinement.

As the sun set behind Bikaner's sand dunes on my final evening before departing toward new professional horizons, its golden light transformed the harsh landscape into a scene of breathtaking beauty—a visual representation of the transformative perspective that desert wisdom provides. This image would remain with me throughout my subsequent journey, a reminder that perception determines experience and that beauty emerges in unexpected places for those prepared to recognise it.

The desert chapter was concluding, but its wisdom would continue illuminating the path ahead—golden light guiding a journey through territories yet unexplored, but approached with confidence developed through challenges already overcome. Whatever professional and personal landscapes awaited beyond the horizon, desert resilience would provide the foundation for navigating their inevitable challenges while appreciating their unique opportunities and unexpected beauty. And unknown to me at that time, a girl had stepped into college in a desert town not far from Bikaner. In another six years, she would be my life partner, embodying the dual nature of the desert, blending beauty and compassion with resoluteness and practicality. She would not only nurture me but also enrich me as the perfect union of masculine and feminine, as I had explained philosophically at the extempore speech competition at Maharani College. The desert had not only nurtured me; it had given me my life!

Epilogue

Horizons Revisited

As I sit on my balcony in Noida near Delhi on an October evening in 2025, watching the sun descend behind the urban skyline, I find myself drawn back to another sunset—the one that painted Bikaner's sand dunes with golden light as I contemplated my first professional role thirty years ago. The physical landscapes couldn't be more different: concrete towers have replaced desert expanses, air conditioners hum where hot winds once blew, and digital screens illuminate what darkness would have claimed. Yet something essential remains unchanged—that peculiar mixture of reflection and anticipation that accompanies twilight, inviting assessment of paths travelled while hinting at journeys yet to come.

At fifty-three, I've lived long enough to recognise patterns in my life's seemingly disparate chapters. The military child who watched fighter jets slice through Jamnagar's skies, the teenage revolutionary who dreamed of reshaping society, the MBA graduate navigating corporate corridors, and the development finance professional designing blended finance platforms for healthcare—these aren't separate identities but evolutionary stages of a continuous self, each building upon and transforming what came before.

My journey began quite literally in the Air Force, born at the Air Force Hospital in Chakeri, Kanpur, in 1972. Those early years under the shadow of wings established the foundation of who I would become. The constant relocations—from Palam to Jamnagar, Amritsar to Adampur, Ambala to Bikaner—instilled an adaptability that would later enable me to navigate diverse professional environments with relative ease. The structured military environment, with its emphasis on discipline, service, and strategic thinking, provided a framework that continues to influence my approach to challenges decades later.

I recall standing on the toilet roof at Ambala, watching Jaguar fighters take off at dusk, their afterburners glowing against the darkening sky. Those moments of pure wonder—the visceral thrill of powerful machines transitioning from earth to sky, the precision of formation flying during air shows, the technical mastery required to maintain and operate complex systems—shaped my appreciation for both technological achievement and human capability. Though I never realised my childhood dream of wearing a uniform, those early exposures to military excellence established standards of performance and purpose that would guide my civilian career.

The nomadic nature of military life taught me to find home not in physical locations but in relationships, values, and internal landscapes that remained constant despite changing external circumstances. This capacity to maintain core identity while adapting to new environments would prove invaluable throughout my professional journey, allowing me to work effectively across diverse organisational cultures while remaining grounded in fundamental principles.

A military childhood also provided early exposure to national events that most civilians experienced only through the media. Witnessing Operation Bluestar from our quarters in Amritsar, observing the aftermath of Indira Gandhi's assassination, experiencing the tension of Operation Brass Tacks—these weren't abstract news items but lived realities that shaped my understanding of how geopolitical forces affect individual lives. This perspective would later inform my approach to development work, recognising that policies and programmes must account for their impact on real people in specific contexts rather than relying solely on theoretical frameworks or aggregate statistics.

Revolutionary Dreams and Academic Realities

My teenage years coincided with significant global transformations that challenged my emerging worldview. The collapse of communist regimes across Eastern Europe in 1989–90 occurred just as I was developing a passionate interest in Marxist-Leninist philosophy, creating cognitive dissonance that demanded resolution. How could systems that promised equality and justice fail so dramatically? What did their collapse reveal about the relationship between idealistic visions and practical implementation?

These questions accompanied me through my academic journey, from the unexpected pivot to the humanities after failing Chemistry in my board exams to my undergraduate studies at Rampuria College and the MBA programme at IMS Bikaner. The revolutionary idealism of my teenage years gradually matured into a more nuanced understanding of social change—recognising that sustainable transformation requires not just a compelling vision but practical mechanisms for implementation, not just a critique of existing systems but viable alternatives that address complex realities.

This evolution didn't represent abandonment of earlier values but their refinement and contextualisation. The concern for justice and equality that had drawn me to revolutionary literature remained central to my worldview, but my understanding of how these principles might be realised shifted from revolutionary disruption towards evolutionary reform—working within existing systems to gradually reshape them rather than attempting wholesale replacement.

My academic experiences in Bikaner provided valuable lessons beyond the formal curriculum. The administrative obstacles I encountered—from missing English Literature papers during undergraduate studies to a missing dissertation during the MBA programme—taught me to persist in navigating bureaucratic systems, a skill that would prove essential in my later work with government health departments and international development agencies. The contrast between theoretical frameworks presented in classrooms and practical realities observed during internships highlighted the importance of contextual understanding and implementation capacity alongside conceptual knowledge.

The summer internship at Pantaloon Fashions in Delhi, with its physical hardships and exposure to corporate hierarchies, created unexpected empathy with the urban working poor that theoretical discussions could never have generated. Travelling through Delhi in a physically depleted state—dizzy from heat, weakened by inadequate nutrition, constantly balancing on the edge of collapse—provided a visceral understanding of the challenges faced by those navigating urban poverty daily. This embodied knowledge would later inform my approach to development economics and poverty reduction initiatives, ensuring that technical solutions remained grounded in appreciation for lived experiences rather than abstract statistical representations.

Perhaps most significantly, my academic journey facilitated the integration of seemingly contradictory identity components developed during different life phases. The military values instilled during childhood—discipline, service orientation, strategic thinking—found expression through academic achievements and group leadership despite a civilian educational context. The political awareness and social justice concerns developed during undergraduate years maintained relevance despite professional preparation for corporate environments, often perceived as prioritising profit over equity considerations.

From Corporate Beginnings to Development Finance

My professional journey began modestly with that first position at the Times of India Group in Bikaner—a role that aligned with neither my academic specialisation nor personal interests but provided a stable foundation from which to begin professional development. This initial compromise between ideal and practical considerations established a pattern that would characterise many subsequent career decisions—balancing personal interests against market realities, theoretical preferences against practical opportunities.

The transition from this first corporate role to positions increasingly aligned with my core interests and values wasn't linear or predetermined but emerged through a combination of intentional choices and unexpected opportunities. My move to the Indian Institute of Health Management Research (IIHMR) in Jaipur in 1997 marked a significant pivot toward health systems—a field that would become my professional home for subsequent decades. This position combined my analytical capabilities with a growing interest in social impact, allowing me to apply financial and economic frameworks to challenges affecting human well-being rather than merely corporate profitability.

The progression from IIHMR to the GTZ-EPOS Basic Health Project in Himachal Pradesh represented further alignment between professional responsibilities and personal values. Working in the Himalayan state whose beauty had captivated me during that brief visit from Ambala years earlier, I found myself applying economic analysis to strengthen public health systems serving vulnerable populations. The role combined technical rigour with tangible social impact—developing costing methodologies for health services, conducting patient feedback surveys, assisting district authorities with strategic planning—creating a professional identity that integrated analytical capabilities with a commitment to equity and access.

Subsequent positions with the Rajasthan Health Systems Development Project, EPOS Health India, the National Health Systems Resource Centre, and the Population Foundation of India represented progressive expansion of both responsibilities and impact. Each role built upon previous experience while introducing new challenges and learning opportunities—from developing flexible financing approaches for the National Rural Health Mission to preparing budget norms for the National Urban Health Mission, from conducting Public Expenditure Tracking Surveys to designing healthcare public-private partnerships.

My transition to the United States Agency for International Development (USAID) in 2016 marked a significant expansion of both scope and scale. The position allowed me to design and implement innovative financing mechanisms that leveraged limited development assistance to mobilise private capital for health initiatives—creating a multiplier effect that expanded available resources for addressing critical health challenges. The Utkrisht Impact Bond for maternal and neonatal health in Rajasthan, the SAMRIDH blended finance platform for COVID-19 response, healthcare loan portfolio guarantees with financial institutions—these initiatives represented practical application of financial innovation to development challenges, creating sustainable funding models that could continue delivering impact beyond traditional grant timelines.

The recognition received for these efforts—Mission Honour Award in 2019, Meritorious Honour Award in 2018, Eagle Award in 2024, and another Meritorious Honour Award in 2025—provided external validation that innovative approaches to development finance could indeed create meaningful impact. More important than these accolades, however, was the tangible difference these initiatives made in people's lives—mothers and newborns surviving childbirth complications, healthcare entrepreneurs expanding access to underserved communities, and health systems strengthening their resilience against future pandemics.

My current role as Director of Innovative Financing at Impact Scale Ventures represents a continuation of this trajectory—applying blended finance approaches to mobilise capital for social enterprises, facilitating access to India's emerging Social Stock Exchange, and conducting impact assessments that measure social value alongside financial returns. This position integrates the analytical rigour developed through academic training with the social commitment that has motivated my professional choices throughout my career.

Looking back on this professional journey, I recognise how seemingly disparate elements of my background have contributed to my effectiveness in development finance. The military childhood that taught adaptability and strategic thinking, the revolutionary phase that instilled concern for social justice, the MBA training that provided analytical frameworks, the early corporate experience that developed practical business understanding—these diverse influences converged to create a professional identity uniquely suited to bridging different worlds and perspectives.

The boy who once stood watching fighter jets take off against Ambala's sunset now designs financial instruments that help social enterprises take flight. The teenager who dreamed of revolution now works within existing systems to create evolutionary change. The MBA student who projected inflation rates for equity research now forecasts social returns alongside financial ones. These aren't contradictions but continuities—different expressions of consistent values and capabilities applied to evolving contexts and opportunities.

Spiritual Dimensions and Personal Integration

My professional journey has been accompanied by a parallel spiritual exploration that has grown increasingly important with passing years. The seeds of this dimension were planted early—watching my father meditate peacefully on the banks of the Ganges during family trips to Haridwar, experiencing the transcendent atmosphere of Durga Puja celebrations at Air Force stations, and glimpsing something beyond ordinary reality during those evening arati ceremonies when flames leapt high after holy water was poured on large diyas.

These early exposures created a foundation for spiritual interest that would develop more fully in adulthood. As professional responsibilities increased and material success accumulated, I found myself drawn toward deeper questions of meaning and purpose that neither career achievements nor intellectual frameworks could fully address. The spiritual traditions that had formed the background of my childhood gradually moved to the foreground of my personal exploration.

This spiritual journey has increasingly focused on the fierce forms of Shiva, Bhairav, and Shakti—manifestations that embody transformation through confrontation with life's full spectrum, including aspects often avoided or denied in conventional spiritual discourse. These traditions acknowledge that genuine spiritual development requires engaging with shadow elements rather than merely cultivating pleasant states—integrating rather than transcending the full range of human experience.

Perhaps most importantly, spiritual perspective helps maintain the connection between technical work and human impact—remembering that behind every data point, budget allocation, or financing structure are real people whose well-being is affected by decisions made and systems designed. This awareness infuses professional responsibilities with deeper purpose, transforming technical tasks into expressions of service rather than merely professional obligations.

The integration of professional capability with spiritual awareness represents an ongoing process rather than an achieved state—continuous balancing of seemingly opposing elements that creates dynamic equilibrium rather than static resolution. This integration extends beyond professional and spiritual dimensions to encompass all aspects of identity developed throughout the life journey.

This integration hasn't eliminated tensions between different aspects of identity but has created the capacity to hold these tensions creatively rather than seeking premature resolution. The ability to maintain multiple perspectives simultaneously—technical and human, analytical and intuitive, practical and aspirational—has become a professional strength rather than a personal contradiction, allowing engagement with complex challenges that resist simplistic approaches.

Full Circle: The Journey Continues

As I approach the conclusion of this memoir, I find myself reflecting on both the continuities and the transformations that have characterised my journey. The physical environments have changed dramatically—from military quarters under flight paths to an urban apartment overlooking a cityscape—yet certain essential qualities remain consistent across these changing contexts.

The capacity for wonder that made me gaze skyward at passing aircraft now expresses itself through appreciation for innovative solutions to seemingly intractable problems. The adaptability developed through constant relocations now enables navigation of rapidly evolving professional landscapes. The discipline instilled through military proximity now manifests as persistence in pursuing long-term objectives despite inevitable setbacks.

My professional achievements—designing India's first Development Impact Bond for maternal health, creating the SAMRIDH blended finance platform during the COVID-19 pandemic, and receiving multiple awards from the United States government—represent not a departure from earlier values but their evolution and practical application. The idealistic teenager who dreamed of a more equitable society has become a development finance professional who designs concrete mechanisms for expanding healthcare access. The military child who admired strategic thinking has become a programme designer who creates sustainable funding models for social impact.

The journey hasn't been without disappointments and regrets. The missed opportunity to pursue a military career through the Short Service Commission remains a poignant reminder of the path not taken. The administrative obstacles that delayed official recognition of my MBA qualification for nearly three decades exemplify systemic inefficiencies I've worked to address professionally. The romantic misadventures of youth—particularly that mortifying episode during the MBA—provide humbling reminders of learning that comes through failure rather than success.

Yet these disappointments have contributed to my development as much as my achievements have. The military career not pursued heightened appreciation for alternative forms of service. The administrative frustrations strengthened my determination to improve systems for others. The romantic missteps have taught valuable lessons about authentic communication, enhancing both personal and professional relationships.

Looking forward from this midpoint of life, I recognise that the journey remains unfinished. The doctoral studies in business finance completed this year represent not a culmination but a continuation of lifelong learning. The transition from USAID to an entrepreneurial venture marks not retirement but a redirection of professional energy toward new challenges and opportunities. The spiritual exploration that has deepened in recent years opens territories for growth that extend beyond conventional measures of achievement or success.

The most significant continuity across this journey has been a commitment to finding meaning through contribution—applying capabilities toward purposes larger than personal advancement or material accumulation. This commitment has expressed itself differently across changing circumstances—from an NCC cadet supporting a struggling teammate during a training run to a development finance professional designing healthcare funding mechanisms—but the underlying orientation toward service has remained consistent.

This orientation doesn't reflect extraordinary virtue but a natural extension of values absorbed during a military childhood, where service to the nation was a standard expectation rather than an exceptional sacrifice. The military community that formed my early environment demonstrated daily that individual efforts gain meaning through their contribution to collective welfare—a perspective that has informed my professional choices throughout subsequent decades.

As I watch another sunset from my balcony—so different from those desert evenings yet evoking a similar contemplative mood—I feel profound gratitude for the journey thus far. The challenges encountered have developed capabilities I might otherwise never have discovered. The opportunities presented have allowed application of these capabilities toward meaningful purposes. The relationships formed have provided both personal fulfilment and professional collaboration essential for creating impact beyond individual capacity.

The horizons I've chased throughout life have never represented final destinations but rather directions of travel—orientations toward possibilities that evolve as each apparent endpoint reveals new territories beyond. The fighter jets that captured my childhood imagination disappeared into distant skies, yet their trajectories suggested possibilities beyond visible limits. Similarly, each professional achievement has revealed further challenges awaiting attention, and each spiritual insight has opened questions inviting deeper exploration.

This continuous unfolding of horizons doesn't represent failure to arrive but recognition that meaningful journeys involve ongoing discovery rather than completion. The development challenges I address professionally aren't problems to be permanently solved but rather complex systems that require continuous adaptation and innovation. The spiritual questions I explore personally aren't puzzles to be definitively answered but mysteries to be repeatedly engaged from evolving perspectives.

In this spirit of continuous journey, I find myself returning to the metaphor that has accompanied me since childhood—flight as a symbol of both freedom and purpose, both individual aspiration and collective achievement. The aircraft that dominated my early visual landscape represented human capacity to transcend apparent limitations while maintaining precise direction—qualities that continue to inspire my approach to both professional challenges and personal development.

Though I never piloted those magnificent machines in person, I've sought to embody their essential qualities throughout my journey—maintaining clear direction while adapting to changing conditions, balancing technical precision with broader purpose, and transforming potential energy into meaningful movement. The specific vehicles for this journey have changed from military aircraft to financial instruments, from revolutionary literature to development programmes, but the fundamental orientation toward purposeful movement has remained consistent.

As twilight deepens outside my window, I'm reminded of another dusk thirty years earlier, watching golden light transform Bikaner's harsh landscape into a scene of breathtaking beauty. That moment taught an essential lesson about perception's role in experience—how the same circumstances can appear either barren or beautiful depending on the perspective brought to them.

This perspective doesn't represent naïve optimism but practical recognition that perception shapes reality—that how we frame challenges influences available responses, that what we focus attention upon expands in significance. The desert taught that beauty exists within the harshest environments for those willing to perceive it, that resources remain available even when not immediately visible, and that extremes inevitably moderate for those with the patience to endure temporary discomfort.

As I prepare to close this memoir, I find myself drawn to poetic expression that captures something essential about life's journey that analytical prose cannot fully convey. The interplay of light and darkness, presence and absence, movement and destination that characterises human experience sometimes requires language that embraces paradox rather than resolving it, that suggests rather than states, that evokes rather than explains.

In this spirit, I offer these words written during a contemplative moment years ago, when watching a sunset over water evoked reflection on life's passages and connections that transcend physical separation:

Sailing through the Dusk

Sailing through the dusk,
Drenched in the molten gold of the setting sun,
Travelling to forlorn;
Where beyond the seven seas
Lives my beloved.
Sweetheart, I travel to Thee.
I see the golden sun,
Your bright face and warm smile.
I feel the darkness enveloping the earth,
The fragrance of your hair.
I rejoice in the warmth of the day just passed.
And dream of the light beyond the dawn to be,
Unmindful of the approaching cold darkness,
Immersed in the here and now
When it is neither day nor night.
I wonder,
Sailing through the dusk.

This twilight space—neither day nor night but a transition between them—has always seemed an appropriate metaphor for the human journey that continuously navigates between what has been and what might be, between memory and anticipation, between achievement and aspiration. The golden light that transforms ordinary scenes into moments of transcendent beauty represents not a permanent condition but a precious temporary illumination that reminds us what's possible when perception aligns with potential.

As I continue sailing through my own dusk—not life's end but its rich middle passage, where accumulated experience provides perspective while sufficient energy remains for meaningful contribution—I remain grateful for the journey thus far and curious about territories yet to be explored. The horizons I've chased throughout life have never disappointed, not because they've been reached but because they've continuously revealed new possibilities beyond apparent endpoints.

The boy who once stood watching fighters take off against Ambala's sunset has himself taken flight in ways he couldn't have imagined. The journey continues, horizons expand, and the view remains worth chasing.